Advance Praise

There is so much to applaud in Diane Helbig's new book, *Succeed Without Selling*. Diane has created a pathway which travels along the new rules of selling that is incredibly well signposted and so easy to follow. The old rules for buyer-seller engagement have been consigned to the annals of history and sadly, whilst buyers have changed the way they prefer to buy, most sellers are still clinging on to approaches and methodology that are now completely redundant. As an example, Diane urges us to forget "Always be closing" and rather focus on "Always be curious" This is a must read for both seasoned frontline sales professionals and students alike.

JONATHAN FARRINGTON, Founder & CEO of JF Initiatives (Top Sales World, Top Sales Magazine & Top Sales Futurists)

P-r-a-c-t-i-c-a-l. That's how you spell the secrets to success by Diane Helbig. Diane demystifies successful sales with advice any small business person can follow. This book is Exhibit A as to why Diane has been such a valued columnist at Small Business Trends—for years! Every small business owner interested in boosting revenue should get this book today!

ANITA CAMPBELL, CEO of Small Business Trends

T0023014

If you aren't closing the sales you want, you might be doing it wrong. *In Succeed Without Selling* Diane gets straight to the point about what works, and what doesn't work in today's marketplace along with tactics you can use to improve your results.

KEVIN KRUSE, Founder and CEO of LeadX

Curiosity and trust are two of the most vital sales accelerators that all small business owners must adopt if they want to win in today's marketplace. But how often do we push aside curiosity just to close the deal? Diane Helbig does a remarkable job of uncovering this critical approach to sales that will shift your mindset from how we've traditionally be taught to sell! *Succeed Without Selling* will open your eyes to the truth about how to sell successfully regardless of industry, business size, or prospect base. I highly recommend it!

**MIKE MOONEY, Driving People Forward,
Author of *Reputation Shift***

A terrific book. With trademark clarity and insight, Diane Helbig teaches the new mindset that is required for sales success in today's business world. The practical yet powerful examples show how to bring this fresh approach to life in any organization, small or large.

SHANE SPIERS, Summit SCALE

It's a new economy. The "Winter" economy as proposed by the late Chet Holmes. Business approaches that worked in the Fall economy will not work in the Winter economy. Diane has done an amazing job of breaking down the sales and sales management process for these times. Her approach is client centric and focuses on how to serve the client rather than how to close them. And by doing so, create long lasting and profitable relationships. This book is a must read for anyone who is involved in the art of selling. And if you own a business, you are selling! Without a doubt reading this book will be a worthy investment of your time!

WILLARD BARTH, Author, Business Consultant and
Transformation Expert

Succeed Without Selling

SUCCEED

WITHOUT

Selling

The More You Think About Selling,
THE LESS YOU WILL SELL

Diane Helbig

NEW YORK

LONDON • NASHVILLE • MELBOURNE • VANCOUVER

Succeed Without Selling

The More You Think About Selling, the Less You Will Sell

Published in New York, New York, by Morgan James Publishing. Morgan James is a trademark of Morgan James, LLC. www.MorganJamesPublishing.com

ISBN 9781642799927 paperback
ISBN 9781642799934 eBook
Library of Congress Control Number: 2020930794

Cover and Interior Design by:
Chris Treccani
www.3dogcreative.net

Morgan James is a proud partner of Habitat for Humanity Peninsula and Greater Williamsburg. Partners in building since 2006.

Get involved today! Visit
MorganJamesPublishing.com/giving-back

Table of Contents

Foreword

By Deb Calvert

Writing a good book is like selling. Both require discipline, creativity, and an abiding belief that you have something special to offer. Both are hampered by self-serving motivations. Both can open doors and provide unlimited opportunities for those who strive to do more than merely producing a result.

When Diane Helbig described her compelling desire to write a book about transcending the negative stereotypes and antiquated approaches to selling, my interest was piqued. After all, her books and podcasts and articles and presentations consistently deliver solid advice about simple, practical ways for SMBs and sellers to increase revenue. *Lemonade Stand Selling* demystified selling for small business owners 10+ years ago. Ever since, Diane has been the voice of reason and simplification for sellers of every stripe, including business owners who don't think of the work they do as *selling*.

Who better, then, to write a book about selling for people who aren't comfortable with sales?

Diane's dedication to genuinely helping small business owners and sellers shows up in selfless ways. She's a prolific writer and contributor to international publications. She's recorded hundreds of podcast episodes that examine every aspect of what it takes to succeed in business. Diane is also "in the trenches" as a consultant and trainer, helping her clients achieve their professional goals and dreams.

Diane is candid. She won't sugarcoat or withhold the truth that can set you free. She'll tell you when you're about to make a mistake, and she'll point out the thinking and behaviors that prevent you from achieving all that's possible. When you've spent a couple of decades watching sellers (including many who are, in Diane's words, "behaving badly"), you spot problems quickly and intervene effectively. When a seller or business owner says "How can I convince them they need my product," Diane frankly responds "You don't." She explains that they're trying to sell instead of trying to meet existing needs. Mindset matters, and Diane works with people on this fundamental first.

When you add it all up, you get *Succeed without Selling,* a book with both practical advice and compassionate, heartfelt support. You get game-changing takeaways for anyone who sells, including those who don't want to sell and those who don't know how to sell.

The subtitle of this book addresses a common misunder-standing: *The more you think about selling, the less you will sell.*

Writer's block occurs in much the same way. If you think about writing, it's not very good writing... you have to think about the reader instead. Diane did. She poured out her heart, spoke the truth, and conversationally addressed the self-inflicted challenges many people experience in selling. She also presented solid alternatives. This is a book about how to sell without being sales-y. It's a book about professional sellership in the modern age. And it's a book that comes from the author's experience, observations, and burning desire to give something of lasting value to others.

Acknowledgments

I am so very grateful for so many people who have contributed to my success, and the completion of this book. First and foremost, I am grateful for my husband, Frank. Without his continued support and encouragement I wouldn't be where I am today. Thanks also go to my kids, Aaron and Macey, for their understanding when I travel and work late. Thanks guys!

I also want to thank my mother Bette, sister Debbie, brother David, and all of my in-laws for their support: Michael, Gerry, Sara, Stan, Jim, Cindy, Dennis, Toni, Marybeth, Jim, John, Dawn, Loretta, and Jim.

I am blessed with an incredible number of friends and associates who have always been in my corner and have supported me in my endeavors over the years. The list is long. As I fear I would leave someone out unintentionally, I am not going to list you here. I trust you know who you are and how much I appreciate you.

I could not have accomplished this piece of work without my awesome editor, Amber Chapman, or my incredible publisher, Morgan James. And my marketing support team, Kristen Wise,

Maira Pedreira, and Dawn Bassick of PRESStinely, are without equal. I am beyond grateful for Deb Calvert for providing an incredible foreword.

I am the businesswoman and sales professional who I am today because of my father, Bob. He taught me so many valuable lessons. I wish he were here to see my achievements.

And, to all of those small business owners and sales professionals struggling to master a sales process that works, as well as those who have figured it out, thank you for being you. I've watched so many of you over the years. This book is inspired by your challenges, and accomplishments.

Thank you my Patron Sponsor, SACS Consulting, Inc. as well as the following people who pre-ordered the book at the Sales Builder Level: Angie P, Ann R, Barbara D, Bonny C, Craig C, Craig Z, Debbie J, Deby L, Tricia B, Diana F, Diane M, Douglas J, Faith S-P, Farnoosh B, Frank A, Harry L, Jan C, Janet G, Jason B, Jessica P, John G, Karen Z, Kate H, Kathleen B, Kelsey L, Laura L, Laura S, Liz R, Marilyn B, Marty M, Megan P, Michael D, Michael S, Michele K, Pamela C, Pat A, Paul N, Bob C, Sandra H, Terese M, Toni M.

Introduction

_____

Whether you're a seasoned salesperson or new to sales, the techniques and processes are the same. And if you're a small business owner *you* are your salesperson. There are things you must do to be successful at sales. How you do them is up to you. In this book, we're going to explore some philosophies, tips, and techniques for successful sales. It's completely up to you to decide how to use these things in your business.

One thing I will tell you is that you can't do nothing and still expect to do well. Sales is an activity that must be practiced daily. It requires a system, measurable outcomes, and effective monitoring. There are also templates in the back of the book and available for download so you can implement the ideas we'll explore throughout this book.

Sales should be enjoyable and something you look forward to doing. If you're reading this and thinking I'm crazy, I'd guess you may be engaging in activities that are antithetical to successful sales practices.

Take a moment to think about what you do as it pertains to the selling process and what your results are. Now, think about how you feel when you're engaged in those activities. If your answers feel like they might be on the negative side, hang in there. This book is going to provide you with an opportunity to shift your mindset, your actions, and therefore your results.

In order to get the most out of it, I will ask that you keep an open mind and seriously consider the ideas in this book; especially if you are not currently getting the results you want.

There is a lot to cover when it comes to sales, so I'm going to explore it in a way that you can take what you need and leave the rest. And for those sales managers out there, I have a special section just for you!

Are you ready to dig into a different, more results-based concept of sales?

Great!

Let's go!

Mindset

"The more you focus on selling, the less you will sell."

Successful sales requires the right mindset. That mindset has nothing to do with selling. Yes, you heard me correctly. Sales isn't about selling! The more you think about selling, the less you'll actually sell. And the more you will struggle.

Before you stop reading, give me a chance to explain. Unless a prospect is in an emergency situation, or you're the only game in town, you don't have a lock on the market. People only buy from people they trust. The best way to build trust is to approach sales from a position of helping others.

Your value as a small business owner or salesperson is how you help other people or companies succeed. When you approach your vocation with an eye toward helping other people it changes the dynamic. Now you're thinking about them. So, it doesn't matter where you are—you could be networking online, or in person. You could be conducting a workshop, speaking, writing an article, participating in a sales meeting, prospecting, engaging with someone at a family function.

Sales is actually about matching a solution to a problem. It's about relationships, trust, problem-solving, honesty, and timing. It's not about convincing, persuading, cajoling, or finessing. Unfortunately, too many people believe the idea that if you're smooth, convincing and say the right thing, the prospect will buy. That might work for a select few. The trouble is that it isn't a practice that works for the vast majority of people and it typically won't work twice. So, those folks may be able to sell to someone once, but they won't be able to repeat it.

Moreover, most people find this kind of sales behavior uncomfortable. If they believe they should be able to sell by persuasion or convincing, but can't, they struggle to close deals. They actually avoid taking the steps they believe they're supposed to. Or they try it but they're so uncomfortable that the prospect is turned off. The prospect doesn't know the salesperson is uncomfortable. The prospect eventually comes to the conclusion that the salesperson is lying.

This is not a good thing! At the same time, the people who are focused on only making the sale, hitting their quota or earning higher revenue are often dissatisfied themselves. They come off as salesy. They are telegraphing their interest in themselves, not on the customer. They don't achieve the sales they are seeking. They flop and lose the sale. The customer is gone.

This is a mindset that isn't sustainable if your goal is to build your business for the long term. If your goal is to gain and keep quality client relationships, I submit you have to have the right mindset.

You must understand that sales will come, and business will grow, but only if you stop focusing on sales. There's an interesting thing about selling that most people don't realize. You have to have a lot of patience. Relationship building takes time. So does networking. Many sales cycles are long, because trust takes time to build.

I tell you this because so many small business owners, sales professionals, and sales managers want quick results. The business owners want to launch a website, and have it drive sales to their door immediately. The salespeople want to attend an event and leave with a new customer. The sales manager wants her team to pound the pavement closing deals.

Unfortunately, this isn't the way it works. You have to accept this reality if you're going to be successful. Sales is a verb. It takes concentration, practice and time. You have to create processes and systems, work those systems, and realize the rewards as they are meant to occur.

Patience is something all small business owners and sales professionals should embrace. Slow down; take the time to be curious and learn. The more a salesperson knows about the people and companies around them, the more valuable that knowledge is. Therefore, the more valuable one will become to their clients, connections, and colleagues.

This acceptance of patience is very important for small business owners who hire salespeople. Having unrealistic expectations of a sales team will only work against you. Set expectations and guidelines that are reasonable, then hold your salespeople to them. This is one way to maximize your success.

Of course, you need to sell. That's a given. But that doesn't have to be your sole focus. As a matter of fact, you shouldn't make it your main focus at all. **The more you think about selling, the less you'll sell.** This is something you'll see repeated throughout this book—it's that important!

Your mindset should be one of discovery, connection, and problem-solving. Embrace the idea that when you have something that someone else needs, and you have built trust with them, they will buy from you. And they are the only people/businesses that should buy from you. Sales isn't about gaining all of the business. It is about gaining all of the **right** business at the right time.

It takes patience and faith; faith that when your mindset is on building relationships, being helpful, and living in integrity, the customers will arrive. And those client relationships will continue for the long term.

Don't confuse patience and faith with waiting. You still must take action and work a process. It's just not going to be the process that was popular in the 1980s.

Here's the bonus—if you're one of those people who hates the idea of being a salesperson, who avoids participating in any aspect of the sales process, then this is the book for you!

We're not going to talk about sales in the traditional sense. We're going to talk about a philosophy and process that I think you'll embrace. And more importantly, that you'll implement.

Still with me? Great! Let's go!

The ABCs Of Sales Have Changed

"Selling should be about discovery, connection, and problem-solving."

Back in the 1980s and 1990s, salespeople were taught a very specific method of selling. The environment was such that the salesperson held the power. Consumers, including company purchasing professionals, did not have easy access to information about the products and services they needed.

There was no easy way to gain insight into new products or upgrades to existing machines, equipment, or processes. The buyer was at the mercy of the salesperson, so salespeople were taught to develop a sales 'pitch' and strategy that could convince someone they needed or wanted the product or service being sold. The more persuasive they could be, the more likely they were to make the sale.

Sometimes that persuasion came across as pushy or coercive. The buyer felt like they were being talked into something or bullied into buying. This is how buyer's remorse happens. When someone is talked into buying something they're not convinced they need or want, or can afford, they then end up feeling bad about the purchase—and the salesperson.

In 1992, the movie *Glengarry Glen Ross* hit the theaters. It became an iconic depiction of the sales industry. "Always Be Closing" became a mantra. Salespeople were trained to always be thinking about the sale. They looked at everyone they met as a prospect. Enter the 'elevator pitch.' This idea was developed around the same time. In short, the idea behind the elevator pitch or commercial, was that a salesperson should be able to spark interest in a total stranger in the time it takes to ride an elevator with them. Salespeople were encouraged to strike up conversations with people in line at the grocery store, at the barber, at school functions. No place was off limits. The focus was to ALWAYS be closing.

There is an argument to be made that this thought process was successful back then because the salesperson was in the driver's seat. I'm not so sure that was the case, though. I think it took a certain type of person to be able to pull that sort of thing off. Many people who tried to become salespeople failed miserably. They just couldn't talk someone into buying from them. It's no wonder that the word 'salesman' developed a negative connotation. Being a salesperson was far less than noble. So, one could question whether Always Be Closing was ever a successful mindset.

Thankfully, once the internet became a household presence, it also quickly became a significant part of the buying and selling process. Now, consumers would have the opportunity to learn about the products and services available to them, not just rely on a pitch from the salesperson. Consumers could now research the companies as well. The seller no longer had the upper hand. Now it had shifted to the consumer. Whether or not Always Be Closing was a successful tactic in the 80's and 90's, it had suddenly become not only ineffective but in fact harmful.

Today the ABCs of sales are: **Always Be Curious**. When you lead with the premise that the more you think about selling, the less you'll sell, you can see that choosing curiosity over convincing is the way to go. When you are curious, you are thinking about someone else. You aren't concerned with yourself, your mortgage or your payroll. You want to genuinely learn about the other person, the company, the situation. There is so much that is good about being curious. First of all, it relieves you of the feeling that you should be the one talking. Because, in all actuality, the opposite is true. You should be listening. And you can't be listening if your lips are moving!

Next, this approach allows you to be present and in the moment. When you are actively listening, you will become more attentive, interested, and engaged. The beauty is that other people will now want to be around you! When you are curious, you are building relationships. You're discovering not only the problem you might be able to solve, but who the person/company is; how do they show up? Do they have integrity? Are your values aligned? Are they difficult to deal with or easy to communicate with? All of these things are important.

Think about it this way—when you bring on a new client or customer, you are, in essence, marrying them. Face it, you're going to be in a long-term relationship with them. So, are they someone you want to deal with every day? Will the marriage be joyful, or will it be unpleasant? The only way to really know is to learn about them. When you are curious, you're open to seeing all of the signs, especially the non-verbal ones. Then you can realistically determine if there is an opportunity to help them.

Additionally, when you're curious you're not assuming everyone you meet is a potential customer, but just the opposite. You're wondering how, and if, they fit into your world. Will they be a resource, a sounding board, a mentor, a partner, a client? Or will they be none of these?

Curiosity means you aren't jumping to conclusions; you aren't making assumptions. And you aren't trying to make someone a client or customer just because you need one. Another wonderful thing about Always Be Curious, is that it takes away the pressure to be persuasive. Heck, it removes any expectation that you're going to do all the talking!

Remember when I said sales should be enjoyable? Well, what is more enjoyable than learning something new, or making a new acquaintance? Sales becomes enjoyable when you stop selling.

Embrace Your Value

"Embrace the idea that when you have something that someone else needs, and you have built trust with them, they will buy from you."

The question isn't, why do people need what you have to sell, the question is—why do they buy it from you. In today's marketplace consumers are in the power seat. They have a wealth of information as accessible as their cellphone. There isn't an industry segment that isn't saturated and competitive. Buyers have a lot of options.

In order to compete effectively, sales professionals and small business owners must be able to answer the question—why do people buy from me.

There are two reasons. The first is they need or want what you have to sell. This means they were already in the market to buy. The second is they trust you. They believe you'll be able to deliver, that you'll be honest and that you want to partner with them. Most importantly, they feel that you care about them.

Nowhere in this set of reasons is it because you've convinced them that they need your product or service. That's because you can't! You can't persuade, convince, or cajole. They won't buy from you because you have the best presentation.

This is tremendously important. When you own this as truth, it changes how you look at selling. And then you realize another truth—you can't sell anything to anyone. You can only build trust and be available with something they need when they need it.

Sounds strange and counterintuitive. You've been raised with the idea that the best salespeople are the ones who are the most eloquent; the ones who do the best job of convincing someone they can't live without the product or service.

If you put yourself in the buyer's shoes you know this just isn't true. As the buyer, the last thing you want is someone trying to convince you that you need their offering. You really want someone to be honest with you and provide you with a true solution—when you need it and not a moment before.

In order to be successful with sales in today's economy you must embrace this concept. It is the foundation upon which you will build your prospecting, selling, and account management processes. If you stick with the old, outdated sales belief system you will engage in sales practices that don't work. When you adopt the beliefs outlined in this book you will build a sustainable, strong business.

This leads me to another really bad sales practice. The prospect wants something in particular. The salesperson, wanting to make a sale, says, 'Sure we can do that.' Unfortunately, if it's not something the company sells, or can do easily, the salesperson has just damaged their relationship with the prospect AND the operations people. The prospect can't trust you now because they don't know when you are telling them the truth. And you are telegraphing that your priority is selling something. It isn't helping them solve a problem.

At the same time, you've just blindsided the operations people. Now they have to scramble to try to create something that may or may not be easy. And they already have a strategy to accomplish their current responsibilities. Phantom products can throw the whole company into a crisis.

Listen, if the prospect wants something you don't offer, ask some more questions. Find out why they want that thing. Then if it sounds like something you should, and could, offer, tell the prospect you'll discuss the possibility with your operations people and will get back with them.

Then, go talk to the folks in your company to explore whether it's possible to offer that product or service. Together you can decide if it makes sense to move forward. Everyone is involved in the conversation, and the decision. So, if it's going to be a thing, everyone will be on board.

The prospect will respect you because you are being honest with them. They'll be happy to give you time to go through the discovery process. They don't want to create a problem for anyone. So, let's not put them in that situation.

Agreeing to provide non-existent products or services won't get you what you want—the sale. That's the best reason not to even try it.

Answer this question—are you in business for the short term or long term? If you are in business for the short, quick hit, go ahead and sell any way you want. Be the salesperson no one wants to deal with. It doesn't matter. Some people will buy from you because they are conflict avoidant and just want you to go away. They think that the best way to get you to do that is to just say "yes."

However, if you are in business for the long term, and want to build something that matters, understand that it takes time to build relationships and trust. It also takes time to build a network around your business that continues to feed you with valuable referrals. So, part of knowing why, is knowing why you are in business to begin with.

There are huge misconceptions out there about sales. While I don't think the ideas ever really worked, I am certain that they don't work now. Unfortunately, many small business owners follow those misconceptions and then wonder why they are struggling.

Knowing why you're in business can be a guidepost. You can refer back to it often to make sure your actions match your goals. If your goals are long term but you're using short term behavior, well, you're not going to succeed.

Your behavior must align with your goals. Always.

Note: Your reason for being in business should not be to make money. You have to be in business because there's a problem you believe you can solve. Money is a byproduct. Henry Ford said, "Wealth, like happiness, is never attained when sought after directly. It comes as a by-product of providing a useful service." Focus on problem solving and the money will come. So, the reason you are in business is to solve X problem for others.

You'll find an example of how to describe why people/companies need or want your offering AND why they buy it from you in the Resources section of this book. You'll also see a download link so you can use the actual document.

Embrace Your Target Market

---

*"Sales isn't about gaining all of the business. It is about gaining all of the **right** business, at the right time."*

Now that you've covered why people buy from you, the question becomes WHO buys from you. Another way to think about this is, who needs or wants your product or service. This is your target market. You may have a couple of target markets. Great!

Example: Jeff owns a company that helps seniors find independent and assisted living opportunities. Two of his target markets are the seniors themselves, and their children. The things that are important to each of those markets might be the same, and might be different. Moreover, the messaging to each of them has to address their main concerns or it won't land.

Make a list of the potential target markets that exist for your product/service. In the next column identify the why—why does that target need or want what you sell. In the next column indicate whether they are a user, a buyer, or both. This information will be critically important when you set out to prospect. You can find a sample form in the Resources section of this book.

As your business evolves revisit this process to ensure you still have the same target markets. Over time you may add services or products that are of value to others. You may decide to drop an offering and thereby remove a target market. A yearly review can be very valuable.

The answer to the question, however, isn't *everyone*. Everyone is not a valid demographic. Everyone DOESN'T need or want what you have to sell. This is another one of those truths that you must embrace to be successful. When you believe that everyone needs your product, you see everyone as a potential client. So, you treat them that way. Your focus is constantly on selling to them.

Ask yourself how you feel as a consumer. How do you prefer to be treated? Chances are good you don't like to be sold. Neither does anyone else. So, if you proceed with the belief that everyone is a potential customer you will treat everyone like a sale. They will feel it, and they won't like it. And then they won't like you. So much for building trust!

Not only is this ineffective, but you end up in business relationships that don't serve you well. You miss the signals others send, letting you know they aren't good customers. If you've ever had a bad client, you know exactly what I'm talking about.

Everyone telegraphs who they are. It's up to you to be open and aware. You can't do that if you have already decided you want to sell them something.

Okay, you've agreed there are specific target markets for your product or service. If you are new to sales or business, you may not have current clients to use as a baseline. So, let's explore this from two different angles.

Let's start with having a client base. We're going to break this down even further and work from business to business as opposed to business to consumer. So, let's start with business to business. Some of those characteristics are: what are you selling them, where are they located, what is their size, what industry are they in, how many people are you dealing with, or how many departments are you dealing with, how many locations are you working with, what is the title of the person you mainly deal with, how do they decision make, how long have you been working with them, how much revenue do you realize with them, and what are the people like that you are dealing with.

Now let's look at business to consumer. The characteristics are slightly different. You still want to know what the person you're dealing with is like, as far as their personality, their values, their viewpoint. You also want to define what you're selling them, how much revenue you are realizing from them, where are they located, what are their demographics like, sex, age, maybe ethnicity; maybe level of education.

Review your current and past clients. Identify the ones you believe are your top 20%. The top 20% are those customers you just love; the ones you really enjoy working with. Now, write down the characteristics of those clients that put them at the top.

In the Resources section of this book you'll see a template for doing this exercise. You'll also find a link to download the document. What you're looking for is similarities between your top 20. What is it about them that separates them from everybody else? It could be what you sell them; it could be how much you sell them, or the revenue that you realize. It could be how much they value what you do for them. What you want to identify is what is it about them that makes them a great client for you.

It's most likely going to be a combination of characteristics. Once you have a picture of this it defines who you're going to prospect toward. It doesn't mean that they're the only people or companies you'll do business with. It **does** mean, however, that this is who you're going to focus on getting connected to.

This is about prospecting; that outward activity you engage in when you are seeking out potential business. When you know what an ideal client looks like, what your best clients look like, it helps you identify who you are prospecting toward.

Remember, this doesn't mean that you are going to turn down business that doesn't meet these criteria. It does, however, help you stay away from the really bad clients; the bottom of the list. You know them. They're the ones who don't want to pay. The ones who complain; who are never satisfied and take up an awful lot of your time for very little money. Those are the ones you're trying to stay away from.

The way you know to stay away from a client, is by knowing the criteria you're looking for because then you can determine how well this prospect is fitting into your expectation. This is why defining your ideal client is so important. In the graphic you will see that there is Ima Winner. Mr. Metoo and Hesa Deadbeat. This is the range of potential clients you encounter.

The truth is that you are shooting for Ima Winner. You'll take Mr. Metoo, and you are hoping to avoid Hesa Deadbeat.

Ideal client

And remember, when you're contacted by a potential client, you can use your ideal client criteria to identify where the prospect falls because you've defined your ideal client ahead of time. This can help you stay out of bad relationships no matter where they come from.

It's important to ask yourself where your top 20 came from. How did you gain them as clients. You've agreed that you aren't going to do business with everyone and that you don't want to. The best scenario is to duplicate who you already have. So, if you know where they came from you can duplicate those efforts!

What does your research uncover? Were your best clients referred to you? Did you meet them at an event? Did they reach out to you through your website?

When you know where they came from you know where to go. See what I mean? You can work hard, or you can work smart. Me, I vote for smart. And smart is to duplicate what works. So, follow the thread backward. Pay attention to who and where. If you discover that many of your best clients come from the same person, work on growing that relationship. Make sure you are taking good care of them, because they are taking good care of you. At the same time, you might discover that someone you thought was a good referral source wasn't. Spending time going down these roads only takes you away from finding good clients. Some people give referrals or suggestions that don't really fit with who your ideal client is. Have a conversation with those people to educate them on what a good prospect looks like. Let them know the challenges you are experiencing with the referrals they are giving you.

Go to the Resources section of this book to see a template for listing those top 20 clients and where they came from. You'll also see a link to access the downloadable document.

The best way to grow your business is to go where you meet the people who can get you in front of your prospects. When you do the discovery around your best clients and work backward to where they really came from you can then create a plan of action. You may find that it's time to change where you network. That's okay. Some things run their course and stop being valuable.

That's why this kind of internal research is a valuable exercise. Commit to doing it a couple of times a year. It will keep you on the right track and ensure that your time and attention are spent where they will do the most good. Start with your best clients and work back.

Now let's explore being new in business and not having a client base yet. This is where market research is critical. You want to uncover who buys your product or service, what their characteristics are, and why they buy it. When you are new to business it can be easy to convince yourself that you have a product or service that is needed or wanted by everyone. Be careful. I get that you've decided to start a business to offer something you think is valuable. It's easy to fall into the trap of thinking everyone should want or need it. Okay, maybe they should. But they aren't going to. The truth is there really are targets you can and should prospect to. Otherwise, you'll end up wasting time trying to sell to everyone and struggling to make the right connections. It's worth the effort to uncover the right markets.

So, build lists of who purchases the items you are planning to offer. If you can, reach out to them to ask some questions. Find out as much as you can about them, and why they need/ want the product or service. This exercise will help you build a vision of what an ideal client might look like. You can add some of your expectations to those characteristics. That will give you a full picture of your Ima Winner.

And let's be honest, while it would be awesome if you could ensure you never get a bad client, that's probably unrealistic. There are times when all of the boxes are checked, you think you've done your entire discovery, and yet, the customer turns out to be a problem. Once you realize there's an issue, you need to do something about it.

Bad clients can do real damage to a company's growth. They take up a lot of time and resources. They're a drain on the enthusiasm and energy of everyone who has to deal with them. All the time spent trying to please that client is time that is not being spent gaining good clients. You aren't doing anyone any favors by keeping these customers.

There is greater value in letting them go. And there are a couple of ways you can do this. You can tell them you're restructuring your business and focusing on a different sector. You can tell them that you've come to realize that you are not the best resource for them. You can refer them to someone else. Whichever method you choose, just do it. Your business will thrive when you aren't engaging with difficult customers.

Now, I know this can be scary. After all, if you don't engage with someone, or you fire a bad client you are losing revenue. That is a temporary situation. Letting go of a bad client affords you the opportunity to replace them with a good, or great client. You will actually be able to gain greater revenue because the time you had been spending dealing with that bad client will now be spent bringing in new business.

So, take some time to get clear on who you should be prospecting toward. Commit to following your path. That means taking a pass on prospective business that doesn't meet your criteria and firing a bad client as soon as you realize who they really are. You have the right, and an obligation, to choose them just like they are choosing you.

Prospecting

"Prospecting is about getting a meeting.
It ISN'T about making a sale."

Now that you know why and who, it's time to think about your prospecting system. One thing to embrace is the idea of targeting a specific market. You've got your ideal client description. You know who is, and isn't, a good client. There's a good chance you have more than one target market.

While that's great, my suggestion is that you pick just one to work on. When you have a single target market, you have something to focus on. And when you have something to focus on, you can create a very targeted, specific message that can be heard by that audience. When it comes down to it, that's what matters.

When you keep your outreach broad, you dilute your message, and no one hears it. This is why so many people struggle with sales. They're trying to rope in too many targets.

No one can get a hold on what the company excels at, who they are, or what solution they really provide, so, no one buys their product or service.

With one target market you can create a marketing message specific to that market. You can speak to the value that a particular target will understand. And your prospecting develops a rhythm; momentum.

Once you have penetrated a target market significantly, you can pull in another one and start the process over again. Now you're working two markets. And so on. When you focus in this way, you find that you'll increase your sales dramatically. The people you're trying to reach will hear you and want to engage with you!

Think about it this way—remember when you were in grade school and the music teacher would have your class sing 'Row, Row, Row Your Boat' in rounds? Somehow she knew the point at which the second and third groups should start. And they started at the beginning, not where the previous group was. That's prospecting to more than one target market. Start with one target audience. Once you've penetrated it to a decent depth, start the next one. Get it?

So, it isn't a matter of NOT selling to everyone who could use your product or service. It's breaking them down into groups and then working on them one group at a time. It's narrowing your focus to grow your business.

A good prospecting system is like a flowchart. 'If this then that' activity mapping can help you know exactly what to do next and when. You get to decide what you feel is the best method for you. Some people choose cold calling. Others prefer to send an introductory letter followed up by a phone call. My preference is to first seek an introduction to the prospect.

That prospecting system looks like this:

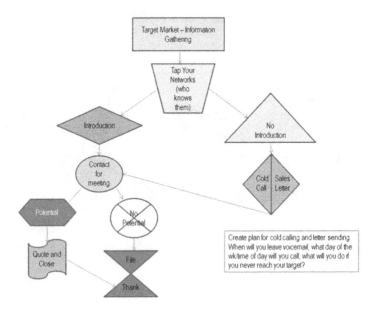

As you can see, once the target market list is created, the first thing the salesperson would do is explore his network to see if anyone can give him an introduction to the target. If so, he would ask for that introduction.

Example:

"Hi Mary. I see you are connected to Dan. I'm wondering if you'd feel comfortable introducing me to Dan. I'd like to learn more about him/his company to see if I might be able to help him."

Your target list will now fall into two categories—those you have a connection to, and those you don't. When you get the connection introduction you will schedule a meeting with that prospect. For the list of prospects you don't have a connection to, you need a process for how you will reach out to them. This is going to be a cold outreach. You may choose to wait until you have a connection. That's okay. Remember to have patience!

On the other hand, if you determine that you don't want to wait until you have those great connections you'll want to create a cold calling strategy that feels comfortable for you. It will most likely be a strategy that combines different communication methods.

There is one prospecting method I strongly suggest you eliminate from your repertoire—emailing. I'm not talking about email marketing. Email marketing can be very effective. That's because it's marketing! It isn't prospecting. Prospecting is different. It's direct outreach to a prospective customer with the specific intent of exploring whether you can help them. And, email is a terrible first step. It's terrible for a number of reasons.

First, it's too easy for the other person to disregard. With all of the viruses circulating, people are very hesitant to open an email from a stranger. Second, there's a good chance your email will go into their spam folder and they'll never see it.

Third, I think it sends the wrong message to the prospect. It gives the impression that you're fishing—casting a wide net hoping something falls into it. Or that you're too uncomfortable to call them so you're taking the easy way. It never indicates a strong desire to connect with this particular prospect. It's just the opposite. It's really impersonal. Besides, it's tremendously hard to start a conversation or relationships via email. If sales is about relationships, trust, and timing, then I think you can see why emailing someone to start engaging with them is not a good idea.

Once you've started a process you can use email as a follow up method. It could look something like this—you call but get voicemail. You leave a brief message about why you are calling. In that message, mention that you are going to send a quick email repeating what you are saying in the voicemail message just in case email is a better communication method for the prospect. See what I mean? Now you can send an email that starts with, 'sorry I missed you today. As I mentioned in my voicemail message I'm sending you this email to share with you why I'd like to connect.'

When a salesperson sees a prospective opportunity as a sure thing, they're setting themselves up for disappointment. Believing you've "got it in the bag" changes the way you approach every conversation. Basically, you stop listening. You're so sure you're going to gain the business, that you go through the motions.

Where does this belief come from? For some salespeople they believe that everyone needs what they have to sell. So, when they network or interact with anyone, they look at them as a sale. They assume the person needs or wants their product or service. They talk instead of listen. Their belief is that they're shooting fish in a barrel and all they have to do is talk about the benefits of their offering. You know the drill; as long as they share enough information in an appealing, articulate way, the other person will jump at the chance to buy.

For others, they're trained to approach every encounter as a sale. They're actually given a "no-brainer" system that, if implemented accurately, will bring endless sales. These systems aren't effective because they don't build trust. They use scripting and language that is transparent. It's obvious the prospect is being "sold." No one wants to be sold anything. They want to buy from people they trust. They can't trust you when you see them as revenue.

One word of caution is to be careful about online programs that promote a sure thing. Not only are these scripted systems, but everyone who buys them is saying the same thing to the same prospect pool. Imagine being the prospect and getting identical solicitations from multiple vendors. It's a total turnoff. And it telegraphs that the seller isn't even bothering to learn about the prospect. They think they've got the prospect figured out, sight unseen.

No one enjoys being treated that way. They don't want to feel like they're just a number. It's like the salesperson is checking the box 'done' and then moving on. Prospects want to feel valued. They want to believe you want to get to know them, their circumstance, their needs. They're more than dollars in the bank.

Moreover, believing the opportunity is a 'slam dunk' can lead to misquoting. After all, you weren't listening to them because you'd already decided they were going to buy from you. Not listening leads to quoting what you 'think' they need/want instead of 'knowing.' The only way to know for sure is to embrace the truth – you don't know whether they are a good prospect or not.

Not listening to a client or potential client is dangerous to your future success. When you don't listen, you miss the signals, the reality, the opportunities, and the times to walk away. One opportunity often missed through slam dunk thinking is resource development. There are a lot of people and companies out there that could be great resources for you. They either provide something your connections could use, or they could be great referral sources for your business. You'll never know if you're looking at them as a future client or customer.

The truth is there's no such thing as slam dunks, sure things, or no-brainers. You don't know whether a person or a company is a real prospective client until you get to know them. The best course of action is to embrace the belief that **nothing** is sure; that your job is to do the discovery.

Get out of sales brain and into curious brain. It's a much better place to be and that's where success really comes from!

When it comes to cold calling, many small business owners would rather clean the toilet than make a call to a stranger! I get it. There is all kinds of mind noise around this. The salesperson finds other things to do. They'll say that they still have research to do. Or they have to button up their marketing before they reach out. Maybe they don't think their website is quite ready for prime time.

Sound familiar? Those sound like valid reasons to wait. However, they become the excuses you come up with when you just don't want to pick up the phone. Understanding what is behind this hesitancy can help you move past it.

Understanding why you are reluctant to call someone is half the battle. Let's also explore what to do about it so you can get past your call reluctance and move your businesses forward.

Sometimes the struggle is with figuring out what to say. You think you have to come up with a compelling description of what you do so the prospect will want to work with you. That struggle could be based in a feeling of discomfort around trying to convince someone to buy from you. Anything you come up with feels strange, unnatural.

Another reason people avoid cold calling is a fear of rejection. There's a lot of psychology wrapped up in hearing the word 'no.' Talk about uncomfortable! The way we process these 'no's is that the person doesn't like us. That sort of blow to your ego can be very unsettling. If you never call, you can never have someone say 'no.' Problem solved!

Both of these issues point to a belief about the call. It says you think the call is where **you** convince the prospect that they need you. You're fearful they'll say 'no' after you've tried to persuade them to buy from you. Yeah, that would be scary! It's also a misplaced belief. The call should actually be the beginning of a discovery process.

The way to approach the call is seeking information from the prospect. You want to ask them a couple of questions to learn more about their situation. Listening to what they tell you will give you the words you need. You will then know how to start sharing your solution. And when it comes to fear of rejection, if you truly have a solution for their problem you will be able to start telling them about it and seeking a follow up meeting to explore further. In the Resources section of this book you'll find some prospecting script ideas.

Remember, the call is simply a first step. You aren't going to sell them anything on the phone. You are seeking to begin a dialog with those prospects who appear to have a problem you can solve. The only way you know if you can, is to ask questions. It isn't to start telling them about your product or service and expect them to connect the dots. The goal of the call is a meeting, not a sale.

I've found that the best cold callers are the people who do their research first. They aren't dialing for dollars. Rather, they are researching the names on their target list to learn what they can. Once they feel like they know enough about a prospect, they reach out to them. Remember that prospecting is about getting a meeting. It ISN'T about making a sale. When your goal is clear—schedule a meeting—it can change how you feel about cold calling. It's easier to ask for a meeting than money, right?

The key is to create a cold calling process that you feel comfortable with, and that has an end to it. So many small business owners ask me how often they should try to reach someone before they give up. That can really depend on a number of factors. Determine how you are going to do your outreach. If you are going to combine calling with email then the number of touches will probably be higher than calling alone. Also, decide the number of days between your outreach attempts. And, have a feel for when you start feeling uncomfortable. At that point, pause your outreach to that prospect and put a note in your calendar to try again in a few months. Wendy Weiss, The Queen of Cold Calling™, talks about using the fourth voicemail as a 'moving on' message. This is where you let the prospect know you believe now is not a good time for them to talk and you are moving on. Give them the opportunity to reach out to you if they actually do want to talk. And let them know you'll try again in a few months.

The more you know about a prospect, the better you can communicate with them, and the more likely they are to respond to you. That's why doing prospecting research is so important. It will also help you become more comfortable when you make your calls.

When you have something meaningful to say to them, it shows the prospect that you are genuinely interested in getting to know them. After all, you've taken the time to learn what you can already.

Consider a couple of things. First, until you actually sit down and have a conversation, you don't know if they indeed are a good prospect. You don't know if you can help them. And you don't know whether you even want to do business with them.

Second, the meeting is about discovery and learning. You simply want to learn more about them, their situation, their needs. At this point, sales doesn't enter into the equation. This is a really important point. If you take sales out of the mix, then all you're doing is meeting someone and getting to know them better. It changes how you feel about the process, about them, and about yourself.

This is the mindset shift I talked about in a previous chapter.

One challenge I see most salespeople and small business owners have is juggling their outstanding quotes with continued prospecting. It goes like this - the salesperson has a handful of proposals out and is waiting for the prospects to move forward. They feel like they had a great meeting; like the prospect is going to buy. They find themselves concerned that these opportunities are going to pop at the same time, so they don't want to keep prospecting. After all, if the business comes, they won't be able to take on any more business for a while.

Okay, hold the phone! It is never a good practice to stop seeking business because you are waiting for someone else to make a decision. Salespeople must prospect consistently in order to succeed.

Here's a simple solution—put an expiration date on the proposal. Something like 'proposal expires 30 days from issuance.' It's that simple. That way, you can continue to prospect and sign the deals with the people who are ready. If someone else finally decides to buy and you're booked, you can refer to the expiration and revise the start date and delivery expectation.

You can also create a statement within your proposals letting the prospect know how you schedule work. When you are clear about the order in which work is assigned, they know what to expect. Setting expectations is a valuable part of any business practice.

Another possibility is you get so busy with work and follow up that you just stop prospecting without realizing it. When you stop, your momentum stops. If you've been doing outreach and suddenly stop there may be situations where you told someone you'd follow up but didn't. Awkward! When you start prospecting again you can feel uncomfortable trying to reconnect with those people/companies. Do it too often and you are shrinking your target market. The more times you go MIA (missing in action) the more people you 'can't' contact again.

Note: If this does happen, just go ahead and reach out to them again. What's the worst thing that could happen? Hit it head-on. Apologize for the gap in outreach and then move on. Often times we make a bigger deal in our heads about this kind of thing than the prospect. There's a good chance they weren't even paying attention! So, suck it up and make the call.

Lastly, it's important to remember that until you have a signed contract or deposit, you don't have the business. It doesn't matter how great the conversation was! So, don't get sucked into the belief that you've got a bunch of business just around the corner. You don't! I hate to be the one to break it to you, but someone has to.

You can't sit back and wait for someone else to make a decision. I don't care how strong your feelings are about the conversation you had with them! If the conversation was really that amazing, it would have ended with a next step. You would know exactly when you were going to start working with that customer.

Remember, you don't want to leave a sales meeting without a next meeting. And if you are at the proposal stage you want to be sure that meeting doesn't end without a *yes, let's move forward*, or a *no, they aren't interested*. *Maybe*, or *they'll get back to you*, just aren't actual answers.

Frankly, if you follow the mindset and process outlined in the selling chapter, you'll manage the process in a way that you should never get to a point where the prospect gives you a maybe, or non-answer.

Use LinkedIn For
Prospecting Research

*"When you connect with people who trust you
and you trust, you can ask them for introductions
to your target market."*

inkedIn is THE professional network on the internet. It is
therefore, a great place to do prospecting research. Doing
effective research requires a plan and process.

Let's start with the value of LinkedIn. Too many people use
LinkedIn to try to sell. That doesn't work. Because LinkedIn is
the place where all the professionals gather, it is the best place
to find connections to our prospects.

Not only can we find our prospects but we can learn a lot
about them through their interactions on LinkedIn. There are
three aspects of LinkedIn to consider when developing a research
process. They are connections, curiosity, and credibility.

Right now we're going to explore curiosity. The more you know about your prospects before you do outreach, the more you will be able to connect with them. The research allows you the opportunity to discover what is going on with them and what matters to them. It gives you things to talk with them about other than what you sell.

Being curious allows you to openly and honestly identify which companies are truly prospects and which you should bypass. Think about what you want, and need, to know about a prospect. It's more than the problem you can solve. You need to know how they do business, what matters to them, what their values are, and more.

So, as you research your prospects, have an idea of what you want to know about them! You can gain great insight into your prospects by researching them on LinkedIn.

In order to be able to research them effectively you have to be able to be connected to them in some fashion. So, let's explore effective connecting strategies. Let's start with your profile. There are some real dos and don'ts here. The first thing to know about your profile is that it should be as professional as possible.

This means having a professional headshot. I don't mean you have to wear a suit if that's not what you wear on a regular basis. I do mean that this isn't Facebook so don't have a picture with your grandkids or dog.

Use your headline to highlight where your expertise lies, not what your title is. This field automatically populates when you add your current job. You can edit it and change it.

Also, add as much to your profile as you can. Your summary is a great place to talk about what matters to you, what you are passionate about, the value you bring to your clients. It shouldn't read like a resume unless you are looking for a job.

Adding as much as you can, includes previous jobs and the high school you went to. This is because LinkedIn takes the information you have in your profile and tries to match it with other people's profile information. LinkedIn can then tell you who you may know. You'll receive some ideas of people you might want to connect with on LinkedIn. And remember, these aren't necessarily prospects. Think about connections as resources.

When you connect with people you know, people who trust you and you trust, you can ask them for introductions to the people who fit your target market.

Joining groups is another great way to build relationships with resources, and possibly with prospects. This is one of the places where credibility comes in. As you engage in discussions and start discussions, you are able to share your knowledge with the other members of the group. And, when you are in a group, the other members are second connections to you. That provides you with an easier path to building a relationship with the ones you feel a connection to.

To get the most out of your engagement on LinkedIn identify your target market. While you can have more than one, I'm going to ask you to pick one at a time. Develop a list of companies within that target market.

Your next step is to identify if you are connected to anyone at the company who can give you an introduction. Using the search feature, search for second connections to either that market or a particular company. LinkedIn will show you who you know and can connect you to the person you want to meet. Don't reach out to the prospect directly. That's a cold outreach while warm introductions work better.

Asking your connection for an introduction to someone you've identified on LinkedIn can look like this: Send an email to your mutual contact and say, "I see you are connected to (prospect). I'm wondering if you'd be open to introducing me to her. I'm interested in learning more about her business and how I might be able to connect her to any resources she may need."

Notice you aren't saying that you want to sell her something. That's because you don't know if you want to sell her something. What you really want is the opportunity to talk with her. Period.

Since you have built trust with your contact she is more likely to say yes. Then you're going to thank her and ask her to do an email introduction. This way, you'll know exactly when the introduction is made so you can follow up.

One other note—send the initial email through your regular email account, not through LinkedIn. Many people don't check their LinkedIn mailbox so they won't see it.

Establishing credibility consists of sharing valuable information in your updates, in your groups, and through articles. Share resources and tools with your connections and prospects. Being in sharing mode helps you do two things. You'll bring value to others which builds trust, and you'll stay out of sales mode (which no one likes!)

Once you've established a connection to the people you want to learn more about, schedule a call or meeting. That call or meeting is strictly for discovery, not selling. Keep an open mind during the conversation. The person you are talking to might end up being a great resource. You won't be able to see that if you are strictly focused on finding customers.

Networking

*"When you change the process though,
you change the results."*

What is networking really all about? Networking is about relationships. It's the act of building relationships with people who may or may not need what you have to sell. You don't build relationships by trying to sell your product or service to everyone you meet. That flies in the face of effective sales practices.

If you start with the idea that not everyone needs what you have to sell, and that there's a lot of people and companies you don't want to work with, then trying to sell to everyone is a waste of time. Add to that the fact that people hate to be sold to. Now, add how uncomfortable it feels to be in sales mode and it's a recipe for disaster, not success.

It's stunning to me how so many people can know the truth yet still behave in a way that doesn't work. I get that salespeople are trained to hand out their cards and gather cards. I understand there are sales managers out there telling their sales associates that productive networking equals walking away with a sale.

It's just not true! The truth is no one cares about your product or service when they first meet you. They don't care about it until they care about you! And they aren't going to care about you if you're trying to sell to them. People want to do business with people they trust. And trust takes time to build.

Therefore, networking takes time. The question I like to ask is—are you in business for the long term or the quick hit? If you answered 'long term' then buckle up and take the time to build relationships. When you first meet someone, you know nothing about them. As you go through the process of developing a relationship with them you will discover whether they are someone who you want to stay connected to. They may end up referring you to others. You may end up referring them to someone else. You may do business together in some fashion. They might just be a great sounding board and contact. Or, they might be awful. Yes, that's right, awful!

You may discover you have no connection with them at all and really don't want to be associating with them. Wouldn't you rather learn that before they become a customer, and a difficult one at that?

Relationships matter in business and sales—even online! Some people think that the internet is for selling. While you all want to sell your products or services, you have to remember that there is one right way and a wrong way to do it. I think some people believe there's a difference because you aren't physically in front of people. We're going to explore that.

I can't express this enough, that the rule of thumb in sales is that relationships come first. If you adopt this idea from the beginning, you will approach the process from the right direction every time. The question becomes how to build those relationships online.

For starters think about what you want in a client. When you have an idea of what a good client looks like, ask yourself how you've obtained the good clients you already have. Most likely you did the work to build the right relationship with them, or with the referral partner first. Go with that policy! You can also refer back to the Embrace Your Target Market chapter where we discuss this in more detail.

When it comes to online prospecting consider these steps. First identify prospective targets. Once you have a target, find out where they are online, and start building a relationship.

Notice that I didn't say anything about selling them. That's because you can't! Just like in-person sales, you need to get to know them and their issues before you can propose a solution. The internet is not your license to email prospects with your pitch. Frankly, that will do more damage than good.

You wouldn't call a prospect and start pitching your product or services, would you? No, of course not! If you called someone it would be to find out about them; to identify what issues they are having that you can help them with. Consider internet contacts in the same way.

The great thing about the internet is that it can give you a window into a prospective client. You can learn a lot about someone or a company by researching them online. Once you've identified them and found out where they are online, reach out to connect and get to know them. Offer them valuable information. Connect them to other resources. Get to know them so you can craft a solution specific to their needs. And if you discover that you can't help them, let them know. You can still continue to build the relationship. They may end up needing you down the road, or they may refer you to someone who does need you.

When you focus on building the relationships instead of on selling something you will find greater success. More people will welcome you into their circle and your good reputation will precede you.

Decide what your goal is. My vote is for a goal of building long-term, lasting relationships that may, at some point, lead to more business. Remember, you may never do business with the person you meet. But if you truly participate in relationship building you just might do business with their connections over time.

You may be wondering what you should be doing if you aren't selling. I find having a strategy helps to prevent falling into the sales trap. The first thing you can do is decide where you should go.

If you belong to an organization be sure you attend the events. You get more out of the groups you put effort into. Put those events on your calendar so you are sure you don't miss them.

When it comes to other events, ask yourself who will be in attendance. Instead of wondering if they are potential clients, ask yourself if they could be good referral partners or colleagues. Since networking is about relationships, decide where you are going to spend your time based on the relationships you could build. I know it might seem like a different way of looking at things—and that's the good news!

Too many salespeople are using networking to sell. That's a short-term view. Those who are looking for long term gains are using networking to engage with people for long term relationships. Think about your own experience. When you attend an event, how do you feel about the people who monopolize the conversation extolling you with the virtues of what they sell; the person who hands their card to everyone? You know the one. She's the person who is so self-focused that she never asks you any questions. She's telegraphing that she has no interest in you at all. Her goal is to get a client. She's oblivious to everything else, including how she is being perceived. Don't be her!

One word of caution: Join philanthropic organizations for opportunities to do good—not so you can sell to the other members. Because, if you are just out to sell to them, that is bad form! The other members will quickly realize your reason for being there. You will negatively impact any opportunity to engage with them when they know your reason is to get business, not to do good. Do good, be a valuable member of the organization, and build relationships. If business arises from the relationships you build there, it's a bonus!

Now that you know where you're going, decide what you want to accomplish. I'll provide the answer to this—to learn something about up to 2 people.

Okay, sounds simple! And that's important. You aren't there to meet everyone. In order to really have a meaningful conversation you have to spend time with someone. Most networking events only last so long. Using your time wisely means giving up on the idea of meeting everyone.

Now, what do you want to learn about the person? I'll tell you what you DON'T want to learn—anything that has to do with what you sell. I'm asking you to leave your business in the car when you go into any networking event. If you're asking questions around your offering, you're telegraphing that you're fishing for business. Your head is still in sales mode.

In order to stay out of sales brain and get into curious brain, select a topic that will give you the opportunity to go behind the curtain and start discovering who the person is.

Some examples are:

What gets you up in the morning?

What are you working on these days?

What do you find most fulfilling about your work?

What, if anything, would you change about it?

These are questions that go to the heart of who the person is. And each gives them the chance to really share. And while these questions are about their job, they aren't "what do you do" or fishing questions about whether or not they need what you sell.

There's more to a networking plan than where you should go and your goal. It's helpful to have a strategy around what you will do when you are there. How will you engage with people? I find this to be the thing that concerns most people. They are unsure how to start a conversation, break into a group of people already engaged in conversation, and get over their nerves and insecurities.

When you get to an event, take a minute to survey the room so you can get your bearings. Take a look around to see who is there. When you walk up to someone, put your hand out toward them and say, "Hi, I don't believe we've met. I'm . . . "

If you're going to join a group of people, you can simply say, "Hi. Do you mind if I join you?" And if you think you're an introvert, be happy about it! Introverts make some of the best networkers precisely because they don't want to be the main person talking. This is where those questions come in to play.

One of the worst questions you can ask is 'What do you do?' That's because when you ask it, the person will tell you. And they will give you their stock, polished, sometimes lengthy answer. Let's be honest—you don't really care about what they do. You should care about why they do it, what joy they get from it, or what made them decide to enter the field. You want to know the result of what they do; how it impacts people or businesses. Moreover, asking someone what they do doesn't start a conversation. Think back to events you've been to and how conversations have played out. Chances are high that you weren't even listening when someone told you their elevator pitch. And they weren't listening to you either! So, why do it? Well, because they happen to be the answers to "what do you do?"

When you change the process though, you change the results.

So, let's change the way you look at, and engage in, the 30 second commercial. For starters, it's not a commercial or a pitch. It's an introduction; a conversation starter. So, the more natural it is, the more comfortable it will be for you to deliver, AND the clearer it will be heard. Get away from the scripted, fancy, and acronym filled jargon. Remove the years you've been in business, awards you've won, and, the how of what you do, or where you're located.

Here's a formula to try:

Your name with

Your company name

Providing X value to Y target with Z result

Example: "Hi, I'm Jane Doe with Your Hometown Insurance Agency. We find out what's important to our customer and then make sure those things are protected. Our customers know they're covered and can focus their energy on other things."

Name—Jane Doe

Company name—Your Hometown Insurance Agency

Value—finding out what's important to the customer and providing insurance coverage for those things

Result—customer has one less thing to worry about and can be present in the moment

It flows, it's natural, and it's plain English. It isn't a pitch. The truth is that you aren't going to sell something to someone in 30 seconds. And you aren't going to sell while you're networking. Your introduction can have a lot of impact on how you connect with people. That connection can be the beginning of a great relationship. Visit the Resources section of this book for more introduction creation options.

As you engage with one or two people make sure you're present and in the moment. Being attentive is extremely important while networking. Remember that you're making an impression on the other person as much as they are making an impression on you. If you appear to be disinterested, they're going to perceive you as rude. Not exactly the result you want!

If you end up talking with someone who is monopolizing your attention without giving you a chance to even participate in the conversation you owe it to yourself to disengage. Don't spend an evening, or lunch, or whatever trapped into listening to someone dray on. There's a difference between having a conversation and listening to a monologue. Some ideas for what to say are:

"Excuse me. I'm sure there are other people here you'd like to meet. I don't want to hold you up." (and then walk away)

"Excuse me. Since we're both here to meet people I don't want to monopolize your time. Let's split up and go find other people to meet."

"Excuse me. I didn't realize how long we've been talking. I promised (a friend) that I'd check in with them. I think I better go find them! And I'm sure there are other people you'd like to meet."

It doesn't have to be awkward. Speaking of awkward, please do not hand your business card to everyone there. Or even everyone you meet. Hand your cards to the people who ask you for them. Those are the people who actually want your card. When you give your card to people who don't want it they don't do anything with it. Or, they add you to their email list. Neither of these are valuable.

Speaking of email lists, please DO NOT add others to your list without their permission. Simply getting their business card is not an invitation to send them your marketing materials. It's invasive and rude. It telegraphs that you are only thinking about yourself. Moreover, it doesn't do you any good to have people on your list who don't want to be there. That's just quantity, not quality.

Storytelling is a key aspect of relationship building. Everyone in your company should know and appreciate the company's story. This includes how the company started, why the founders started it, the problem they saw that they wanted to solve, and what success looks like. It can also include the value the leadership sees in the staff; the impact they believe the staff makes to the clients and the community.

This isn't something that should be scripted. When the leadership shares the story consistently it resonates with the staff. They are then able to tell the story in their own words. This is really important in sales. If the salesperson tries to tell a scripted story, or is told to do so, she will probably come off as inauthentic. Building trust will be impossible.

Storytelling is something you just can't fake. You have to believe the story; it must have meaning to you. That way you can make it your own. And THAT is what will connect with the person you are talking to.

At the same time, be curious about someone else's story. The great thing about asking someone to share their story, is that the story they tell gives you insight into what matters to them. You can learn a lot about a person, or a company, by listening to their story.

Know your own story as well. If you are the owner, what is your motivation? Your passion? If you are an employee, why did you decide to work for your company? What is it about the company that resonated with you?

Now, there's the follow up. Don't spend time networking if you aren't going to follow up with the people you meet. If it's someone you feel a resonance with, invite them to coffee, or offer a follow up call to continue the conversation. If it's someone who you don't feel a connection to, send them a handwritten note telling them it was nice to meet them.

Follow up doesn't include expecting referrals or giving them. Frankly, you don't know the other person well enough to give them a referral; and they don't know you. Expecting someone to start referring you after an initial conversation is not only presumptuous, it's dangerous. When you first meet someone, you don't know them. You don't know their work, their business practices, their beliefs. Imagine what could happen if someone who isn't terribly good at what they do, or respected, starts referring you to people. Suddenly, you are potentially guilty by association. It could ruin your opportunity to make a good first impression.

The flip side is you referring them to one of your connections. What would happen if you did that only to discover that the person isn't good at what they do? How does that make you look to someone in your orbit who trusted you?

I prefer the 60-day policy. This policy states that you do not refer anyone you meet during a networking event for a minimum of 60 days. During those 60 days, you work on the relationship. This gives both parties the opportunity to determine if they should be in a business relationship of any sort. You may find that while you initially liked the person and thought there was opportunity to work together or refer each other, you've determined that you really don't want to pursue an ongoing business relationship with them. It may be that you don't like the way they do business. Or maybe they are so new in their business that you don't feel comfortable referring them to anyone. The point is that just like dating, you have to invest the time in order to know whether you want a casual relationship or something more serious.

Another part of the policy should be a limit to the number of resources you maintain in any given field. For example, you can say that you like to keep 3 graphic designers in your toolbox. Then when you encounter someone with a need you can give them all three names and let them determine who they like. This provides a buffer for you. If you get to know someone, like them, but not their work, this resource limit gives you a reason NOT to add them to the list.

These kinds of policies take the personal and the emotion out of the situation. It's not about them—it's about your business practices. You show up as a professional who takes every relationship seriously, whether it's with a prospect, a client, or a referral partner. That level of professionalism keeps you out of trouble and elevates you in your network. And when you can state this policy easily and clearly, it really becomes a part of your business structure.

Being a good networker isn't about being liked by everyone you meet. It's about being respected. Having policies and best practices builds respect.

One side note I'd like to mention is that you may find yourself quickly building a relationship with someone whose work, ethics, professionalism, and business practices you like. You may want to start referring them before your time frame is up. That's okay! Go ahead! The point is that you've established a system and you're working it. You've given yourself time and space to realistically evaluate the other person. THAT'S what the policy allows you.

So, start with a 60-day policy and see how it works for you. You may decide to adjust it up or down. That's okay. As long as you have some sort of program that you follow, you'll be in a better position.

Attending an event or convention is a great way to gain knowledge, find resources, and meet people. You are taking time **out** of your business to work **on** your business, so you want to maximize the experience. There are ways you can engage with other attendees that can add value to your business. Let's explore some of those techniques.

Networking is always about getting to know other people and building relationships. In order to do that you have to be more interested in learning about them than you are about telling them about you. Care about who they are, care about their experience, and care about their business. That's how they'll learn to care about you.

When you care about others more than yourself it is apparent. And people are attracted to that. One of the best things you can do is to approach someone who is sitting or standing alone and engage them in conversation. They're most likely the person who is there by themselves, is somewhat shy, and uncomfortable with starting conversations.

The best way to let people know that you care and want to get to know them is to ask them questions. Open-ended questions that provide you a look behind the curtain are the best. So, give some thought to what you would want to know about someone. Some suggestions are:

What brings you to the event/conference/convention?

What are you hoping to gain from being here?

What led you to enter the field you're in?

What is your favorite thing about your business?

What does your ideal client look like?

Who have you heard speak so far? What did you enjoy about their presentation?

Whose presentations are you planning to attend? Is there something you're hoping to learn or discover there?

What do you find to be the best client attraction tool you use? (another way to ask this is: How do you gain clients?)

You can see that these are questions that are non-threatening and get someone to share. How they answer tells you a lot about what matters to them as well as what is going on in their business. As you ask questions, listen without assuming or anticipating the answer. Avoid thinking about the next question you want to ask. The goal is to have a conversation. That requires true listening and responding. If, as you listen, you discover that you may know someone or something that could be helpful to the person, tell them. People love a resource! You can start great business relationships by being very present and engaged as you ask questions.

Make sure you follow up. It is one of those things that people often miss. The energy and enthusiasm they feel at the event falls away the minute they get back to work and back into the day to day. However, this is really probably the most important part of networking. Think about it. What's the point of meeting people at the event if you aren't going to continue nurturing the relationship?

This is a place where systems are valuable. An effective system includes deciding how you are going to follow up with different people, adding their contact information and notes to a CRM system, and using a calendar to schedule the follow up activities.

Some follow up options include:

Sending a handwritten note to the person

Requesting a meeting over coffee or via phone to continue learning about them

Calling them to follow up and hear how they enjoyed the event overall.

You may do different things with different people you met, depending on how you engaged with them. Whatever you choose, make sure you schedule the activity on a calendar. You want to be sure you take action. Don't let 'busyness' get in the way!

Frankly, if you meet more than 5 people when you network you won't remember the conversations you had with them. However, that doesn't mean they aren't worth remembering. Using a CRM allows you to keep the information without having to keep it in your head.

Not now follow up: many times when we prospect we encounter a company or person who isn't interested in our product or service. There can be a lot of reasons why this is the case. And while there are times when this is a flat 'no' there are most likely more times when it's 'not now.'

Develop a follow up process for these non-opportunities. Put your notes in your CRM and an appointment on your calendar for reaching back out. This way you can let it go without forgetting all about them. Unless the company closes or the person dies, 'no' is not really forever. That's why it's important to have a system for following up down the road.

Selling follow up: when you are in the selling conversation you are identifying whether the prospect is someone you want to work with, and can help. If your determination is 'no' have a clear and specific process for handling that. This way you stay consistent and don't have to invest a lot of thought. There's no downside to having a script here. Keep it polite and professional. State it or email it. Record it in your CRM and move on.

Have a plan to engage, question, and follow up with people you meet at a convention or event. Decide what you want to learn and who you want to meet. You'll get more from the event than the educational and inspirational opportunities.

One **note** of caution: If you attend a conference or tradeshow, be careful how you engage with the vendors on the tradeshow floor. They've invested time and money to connect with potential clients. Be respectful of their time. Don't fake interest in their offering just to get a chance to see if they might be a prospect for you.

All of these rules apply when you're a member of a referral group as well. There are a lot of opportunities to participate in a group where the focus is on providing and receiving referrals.

The first thing to do is find a group that makes sense for you and your business. If you sell business to consumer you might want a group with other b2c businesses. For those who sell to businesses, it's probably most worthwhile to join a group with other b2b companies. My belief is that the people in the group are then thinking along the same lines and are interacting with the kinds of people you need an introduction to.

Do your homework; visit a couple of groups to see where you feel the most comfortable. Beware of joining a group just because a friend recommends it. While that group works for them, it might not be the right place for you.

Once you find the group you want to join, realize your job is to get to know the other members. Arrive to meetings on time, actively listen to what people say about their business and their needs, and schedule outside meetings with each member. These meetings are NOT so you can sell them your product or service. They are designed for you to learn more about the other person.

When you are in curious brain instead of sales brain you are genuinely interested in others. You know that in order to gain referrals you need to be giving them. And, you also know that you can't give referrals to anyone you don't know and trust— even in a referral group.

Moreover, don't expect to give and get referrals from everyone in the group. It doesn't work that way. There will be people who offer a product or service that your connections need. And there will probably be people whose offering is not needed by the people you know. Example: I was in a referral group for years. I had developed great relationships with the members. One of the members actually became a good friend of mine and is to this day. Even though we know and trust each other implicitly, I was never able to refer her to anyone. I just didn't know anyone who needed her service. She had a very specific niche she worked in.

Another important thing to embrace is that referral sharing is not a one for one proposition. When you give someone a referral don't expect to get one back. If you are thinking that you will gain referrals just because you give them, you will be unhappy with your results. Focus on building the relationships and let referrals happen naturally. When they are authentic, they are more likely to turn into business.

One thing I see people do in referral groups is have expectations without efforts. They think they can join, ask for referrals and get them, period. Not only does it not work that way, but they get the opposite. Remember, people telegraph who they are and what they care about. When someone doesn't give referrals, doesn't listen when other people speak, and doesn't take the time to really get to know the other members of the group, they are telegraphing that they are in sales brain. They are only interested in what they can get. This will be obvious to the other members and this person will get nothing.

Have you ever joined a group and had someone ask you to meet to get to know each other better, but then when you get to the coffee, they start pitching their product or service? Unfortunately, this happens all the time. It's off-putting and does real damage to their reputation. It's not a path to success.

Focus on discovery; be curious; choose to give. And take the time to get to know the other members. THIS is a path to sustained, prolonged success.

One word of caution—you are not supposed to be trying to sell to the other people in the group. The point of these groups is to build relationships with the other members, so you have a degree of mutual trust. Then, they're available to you as resources for your connections, and you can receive referrals from them. If someone in the group decides to do business with you it's a bonus. However, if you focus on trying to sell to the people in the group you will instead alienate them. Your participation will feel awkward and people will avoid you. Remember—no one likes a salesman!

Focus on being a giver. That'll keep you from being salesy, and it'll help you be genuinely interested in learning about others. That's the kind of engagement that builds respect and trust. Be on time, pay attention to what others are saying, and be specific with the referral requests you share. People can't help you if you're too general.

Let's talk some about speed networking. This is one of the most misunderstood activities in the business world today. The belief is that you are going to **connect** with a large number of people. That's just not true. You will have a **very short introduction** to a large number of people. And that's it.

Speed networking is touted as an opportunity to gain referrals from a lot of people because, after all, you are going to meet everyone at the event. It is structured so that everyone meets everyone. Many organizations also provide the attendees with a process for sharing what they are looking for in a prospective client. The expectations is that you will share what you need/want, the other person will make a note of that, and will then connect you to your prospect.

The problem is that no one refers someone they don't really know. And you can't get to know someone in 1-2 minutes.

It's just crazy. What's equally crazy is that people convince themselves they've made great connections and will be receiving referrals shortly after the speed networking event.

Going with our premise that the more you think about selling the less you will sell, speed networking is more activity than productivity.

But is it a waste of time? I used to think so. And, truth be told, it might be. The question is whether there is a way to make it valuable and productive. Well, I think so. If you apply the curiosity test, speed networking can be the beginning of some potentially good business relationships.

When you attend your next speed networking event implement the following practice:

Listen to the other person and ask them a question that can shed light on how they think. Here are a couple of questions you can ask:

What qualities do you look for in a potential client?

What do you value about your best clients?

What qualities do you look for in a company you feel comfortable referring?

How they answer the question tells you a lot about who they are. Then, when it's your turn, give your short introduction and add what you look for in a referral partner—not what prospects you are looking for.

The best way to take advantage of speed networking is to consider who you want to continue a conversation with. The real value is in identifying who resonates, and who doesn't. Speed networking can be the start of a relationship building process. But only if you look at it that way.

Your choices are that you look at speed networking as an opportunity to gain referrals or as an opportunity to meet a lot of people and weed them down to a handful you'd like to invite to coffee.

Since you aren't going to gain referrals from anyone in the room, spend your time identifying those people who you'd like to have a longer conversation with. Mark those business cards so you can follow up after the event.

And then follow up. Reach out via email indicating how much you enjoyed meeting the person. Suggest getting together for coffee in the coming weeks. And when you meet for coffee, continue your discovery process to learn as much as you can about the person. If they are eventually going to be a referral partner, you have an obligation to your business and your connections to know as much as you can about them.

Trust is the key. You can't trust someone you just met or talked to for 2 minutes. In addition, if everyone at the speed networking event is focused on gaining referrals they aren't listening to anything you are saying. They are totally focused on telling you what they need/want. That's why I believe you are better off simply seeking to discover those people you feel a level of connection with. Take it from there.

Strategic Alliances

"Just like selling, you are exploring whether you can and want to work with them."

It's a great idea to find companies that prospect toward the same target audiences you are working with. The challenge is not jumping into a business arrangement until you've truly built the relationship.

Story: Beth owns an accounting firm. Her focus is working with small businesses and startups. She realizes that business bankers, business attorneys, and business insurance providers are all talking to the same prospects. And it gets even better. They are all talking to the owner about the way they help the owner and the business.

Beth decides that she needs to find a business banker who can send her referrals. She knows she has a service that is critically important to the banker's clients. And she knows she's very good at what she does. She's built a reputable business over time.

Beth believes that when she finds a business banker who is working with companies that look like Beth's client base the banker should welcome her with open arms. It's as if Beth has shown up to provide a missing link for the banker.

Okay, hold on. There are too many assumptions here. Assumption 1—the banker doesn't have an accounting firm he trusts and refers to clients. Assumption 2—merely being an accountant is good enough. Square peg, square hole. Not exactly.

Truth 1—Beth has no idea what sort of resources the banker already uses. And Beth has no idea whether the banker is interested in providing accountant referrals to his clients. Truth 2—The banker doesn't know Beth from Eve. He has no reason to refer anyone to her, simply because she's an accountant. Truth 3—The banker might not be very good at banking. He might be difficult or unpleasant. So, Beth might not want to be in a relationship with him at all, regardless of the referral opportunities.

So, what's an accountant (or anyone else) to do? Start with the research around who is also talking to your target market. Once you identify the types of businesses, find some owners or sales representatives who look like they might be valuable connections. Set out to start a conversation. And that conversation should revolve around getting to know them. Don't start by telling them what you do, who you do it for, and the value you think you can bring to their clients. That's all about you. And no one cares about you! At least not until they trust you.

Instead, seek to learn as much as you can about them. Just like selling, you are exploring whether you can and want to work with them. One key element is whether you think you'll be able to provide them with referrals. It's not about you! It's about how you give to your clients, connections, and associates.

Forget about selling; forget about getting referrals. Build relationships where it makes sense and the referrals will come. Strategic alliances take time and attention. You both have to agree on what the relationship is about. Don't jump into it. That just doesn't work.

This is one of those situations where your brain should be in curious mode, not sales mode. I know, you aren't trying to sell to the alliance. However, you ARE trying to get them to refer you to their clients. That's a sales move and mindset.

Remember that until you really know the prospective alliance, and they really know you, you have no idea whether there is a fit. So, treat these relationships like you do every other one. Get to know them, see if there's a relationship to be had, build trust, and then it will make sense to refer each other.

Which brings me to another thing. In my story above, Beth wasn't thinking at all about how she might be able to help the banker. Or how she might be able to help her clients and connections who might need a banker. She was only thinking about what she could get out of the deal. That's never a good idea. Those who focus on giving are the ones who get.

So, when you are looking for a strategic alliance, think about who you feel comfortable referring to your connections and clients. Once again, you don't know until you get to know them. Another reason why the discovery process is so very important.

Next time you are looking for a strategic partner, try this process: Look for someone who fills a need your clients have where you don't offer a solution. Seek to get to know them so you can determine if they are really worth referring. Are they trustworthy? Are they reputable? Are they ethical? Do they work with clients like yours? Do they believe in providing their clients with resources outside their expertise? As you go through the process of getting to know and trust them, they'll be doing the same thing with you. And if they, like you, find value in having an arsenal of resources they can provide to their clients and connections, you'll be referring each other whenever it makes sense.

That's how you'll build valuable, long-term strategic alliances.

Getting and Giving Referrals

---

*"Effective referral relationships are based on
respect, trust, and timing."*

Referrals are a funny thing. They can be uncomfortable to ask for and get from clients. They can be really valuable or damaging, depending on how you engage and who is involved. When you think about it, there is a lot to the art of referral sharing. Effective referral relationships are based on respect, trust, and timing.

There is a level of respect that must exist between the parties in order for any referral sharing to happen. Let's use Joe, Beth, and David for our example. Joe asks Beth for a referral to David. The first thing Beth will consider is how much she respects Joe and the way he works. Interestingly, Joe should be considering how much he respects Beth as well. And he should decide before he asks her for that referral.

You want to be sure you are affiliating with people you respect, and not with anyone else. It's your reputation that's on the line when you refer someone. Your connections are treasures and you should be protecting them. In order to be able to effectively refer, and receive referrals, you first need to take the time to build those relationships.

There's a trust triangle that's created when people refer each other. Beth isn't going to refer anyone to David who she doesn't trust, because David trusts her. And, when Beth refers someone to David, she has an expectation that they are going to treat David well. If they don't, she won't refer them in the future. She can't afford to. A bad referral to David can negatively impact her relationship with David moving forward. It's also going to negatively impact her relationship with the person she referred.

If you refer someone to one of your connections and they don't deliver, are you going to refer them again? Probably not. If you do, you're definitely going to give it a lot of thought before you decide.

When you decide to ask someone for an introduction be sure you trust and respect them. You are sometimes evaluated by the company you keep. If the person you're asking isn't trusted or respected, their referral isn't going to mean much.

This is probably the most interesting part of referral sharing. There's a right time, and way to ask for a referral. You can't expect someone you've just met to refer you to anyone. Moreover, you shouldn't be quick to refer someone you've just met. Take time to get to know them, trust them, and respect them. Only then can you comfortably engage in a referral relationship.

When it comes to your customers, timing is really important. You shouldn't ask for a referral from them until you've done a great job for them AND have developed a respectful relationship with them. They have no stake in referring you, so expecting them to do it naturally isn't going to get you very far. Once you've established a great relationship with them, that's when you can ask if they know anyone who could use the solution you provide. And, asking if they'd feel comfortable making an introduction is a nice, gentle way to do it.

After all, they might not feel comfortable with referring. Some people don't. And that's okay. The last thing you want to do is make them feel uncomfortable.

Selling

"The more you think about selling,
the less you will sell."

There are two different avenues of selling. One is toward new clients and the other is deeper within a current customer. Let's start with new.

To keep things clear and straightforward, think of selling as the activity you participate in when you're in front of the prospect. In previous chapters we covered your value, who it's valuable to, prospecting, and networking.

We talked about seeking to get the meeting, not the sale. That's what prospecting is all about. Remember, until you've had a chance to learn about the prospect, you don't know whether there really is an opportunity.

Unfortunately, what often happens during the sales meeting is the salesperson talks, and talks, and talks. This is where the salesperson thinks they are supposed to show their presentation, talk about the benefits of their product or service, and wow the prospect into being eager to buy.

Then they're amazed when that isn't the result of the meeting! Well, of course it isn't. The more the salesperson is talking, the less the prospect is listening. If the point of prospecting is getting the meeting, the point of the meeting is discovery.

Your goal should not be to tell the prospect all about your product or service. It should be to learn as much as you can about the prospect. When they ask you to tell them about what you sell, tell them you'd love to but first you'd like to ask them some questions so what you share is relevant to their needs. Then start asking your questions.

Really listen to what they tell you and take notes. You are building a picture of the prospect, their need, their business practices, their decision-making process, what matters to them most. As you listen you are determining two things: whether you can help them and whether you want to.

Depending on how they answer, you may discover that you can't help them. Maybe their situation is beyond the scope of your offering. Maybe their budget is too small. At the same time, you may discover that they are not a good fit for you. If they are not forthcoming with answers, they don't want to work with you. I know that sounds harsh. Sometimes the truth hurts.

Let's play it out. You've secured the meeting and are sitting with a prospect. It's easy to assume this means the prospect is interested in possibly working with you. At the least, they want to learn about your offering. Okay. Great! And breathe.

Instead of telling them about your product or service, you are going to do your discovery and ask them questions. If you find that the prospect is not giving you answers freely, there's a disconnect. When someone is interested in exploring whether it makes sense to enter into a business relationship with you, they want to give you as much information as possible so you can provide them with valid solutions. They know that the more forthcoming they are the easier it is for you to connect their situation to your solution.

Unfortunately, the opposite is equally true. It's just a truth of sales that you are wise to embrace. Someone who withholds information or is a stingy communicator is telling you they don't trust you—yet. Or they really aren't interested in working with you. For whatever reason, they are going through the motions.

You can see why it is so very important to be curious instead of sales-focused. When you're curious you are present, aware, attentive. You will identify positive, and negative, behaviors easily. Believe me when I tell you that embracing this idea will hurt less than taking on a client who turns out to be difficult. The whole point of the sales meeting is to make sure there's a good fit. You are both interviewing each other.

Too often the salesperson puts all of the decisions on the prospect. They fail to realize that they have a say as well. We're talking about being successful. If you consistently take on difficult customers, you are going to struggle to succeed.

Think back to your current and past clients. Think about the ones you just love, and the ones you just hate(d). For now, let's explore those you hated. What was it about them?

Did they beat you up on the price?

Did they fail to share pertinent important information that created more work for you?

Did they complain often?

Did they take up a lot of your time?

Were they indecisive?

Were they slow to pay?

Guess what? If you had asked enough questions during the sales meeting you probably would have identified these issues and could have avoided the problems all together. Let's be honest. You're usually so focused on gaining revenue that you ignore the signals the prospect is sending you.

You either don't ask enough questions, you disregard the answers or the way the questions are answered. And then suddenly, you're upset with them once you start working with them.

You have an obligation to your company, and your current clients, to fully vet a prospective client. That vetting requires your full attention and honesty. Some of the questions you should be asking are:

What's your decision-making process?

Notice I didn't say 'Are you the decision maker?' You need to know how they make decisions but asking if the person you are speaking with is the decision maker is rude. Not only will they say 'yes' whether they are, or not, but they'll be offended. When you ask the question above you are simply seeking information. There's no reason for anyone to get defensive.

Have you used a product or service like this before?

You want to know what their experience has been. If they say 'yes,' you can follow it up with questions about that experience.

Those questions can include:

What did you like about the vendor?

What, if anything, would you change if you could?

If they are still working with the vendor, you want to know why they are looking for a replacement. If they stopped buying the product or service, you want to know why.

If they said 'yes' to the above question you can ask them what their typical monthly or annual spend was or is. That gives you an idea of what their budget might be. At least you will know what they are spending or have spent in the past for the same thing.

If they haven't purchased the product or service in the past you can ask:

Have you considered a budget for this?

It's a less threatening question than 'what's your budget?' Prospects don't like to share what they are thinking regarding what they'll spend because they fear the salesperson will price up to that amount. Understanding this gives you an opportunity to connect with them. When you then ask them if they've considered a budget you make it easy for them to answer. All of these questions continue to build trust. The prospect can see that you are really interested in gaining information so you can do your best at providing them with information.

If they're still reluctant to offer information you can say something like: "I get it that sharing a budget can be scary. My goal is to be sure I have enough information to accurately assess if and how I can help you. Would it help if you talked about a range? I can tell you that an investment in our services can range from x to y. The level of service we'll be able to provide also fits that range."

When you have the budget conversation after you've asked all of your other questions you should have a pretty good idea of what they need, and what you can do for them. At this point you can provide them with an idea of what the max might look like. And you can ask them if that is out of their reach. You really need to know this. There's no point in going any further if their ceiling is significantly lower than what they'd need to spend.

Here are some more questions that can be valuable:

What is your timeline? (Is there a sense of urgency for that client?)

What will success look like?

What is your preferred method of communication?

These are questions that are beyond the ones you need to ask about the specific situation. You'll want to add those questions to the list. Once you have answers to everything, you'll know whether you can and want to work with them.

If the answer is no, you can't or won't work with them—tell them. Thank them for the information and tell them you don't believe your company is the best resource for them. You can refer them to other providers if you want. Believe it or not, turning down business builds trust.

If the answer is yes, you feel that you and they are a great fit, and you'd like to work with them, thank them for the information and tell them you believe based on what you heard, that you can help them. Tell them you'd like to review the information and put a proposal together. Ask them for a meeting no more than a week out, when you can bring the proposal and review it with them.

You never want to leave a sales meeting without a firm next step. Prospects will ask you to email the proposal. That's not the best idea. You want to be with them when they get it so you can review it with them. That way you can answer any questions they might have.

If it's not geographically possible to give them the proposal in person, you'll have to email it. You still want to have a call on the calendar for reviewing the proposal.

If you leave the meeting without a next one scheduled, you might fall into the trap of not being able to get them on the phone. Or waiting for them to contact you. Either way, you've lost control of the situation.

Here's one very important thing to keep in mind; when you are asking good questions and really listening to the answers, then responding with a proposal that speaks only and exactly to what they told you, the odds of being confronted with objections go way down. That's why the discovery process is so very important.

By responding to what you heard them say you are showing them that you heard them and are providing them with a solution. This is why a proposal with review meeting is so important.

The proposal should include a summary of what you think you heard. The next section is where you spell out what you'll do and relate each part back to the summary. When you provide the connection, you make it easy for them to follow.

During the review meeting you'll share what you think you heard from them in the first meeting. This gives them an opportunity to tell you if you misheard them, or if something changed. The continued dialogue is what's important.

As long as you've addressed everything they told you, there's no reason they shouldn't agree to do business with you. You can find a proposal template in the Resources section of this book.

What is included in your list of questions? Head to the Resources section of this book to find a list of discovery questions. I went ahead and got you started. From there you can visit the website to download the list for your own use.

Now let's explore how to gain business from current clients. This is one of the best avenues of new business and unfortunately, is one that is often missed. We've got this idea that salespeople are supposed to be hunters. You go out and gain a client and then move on to the next conquest. This tends to leave your current clients alone and unattended.

The crazy thing is that many times there's more business to be had with current clients. But, instead of pursuing that business, you convince yourself that your clients know everything you do, and they'll contact you if they need you. Well, guess what? They don't know everything you do. Hopefully, you didn't try to tell them everything you do when you were in the sales meeting! And if you did, they wouldn't have heard it because they weren't interested in everything you do. They were interested in the one thing they needed.

So, there's value in reconnecting with your clients over time. You want to continue to nurture the relationship. You want to know what's going on with them so that you can offer resources—either your own or those of a referral partner. Spending time with your current clients is one of the easiest ways to grow your revenue. They already know you and trust you. They'd rather do business with a company they know than have to take a risk with a stranger.

At the same time, if you aren't paying attention to them, it's pretty certain your competition is. If they are there when the client needs something, and you aren't, the competition will most likely get the business.

You shouldn't convince yourselves that your clients will be loyal to you. They have no reason to, so it's up to you to give them reasons. Caring about them and their success is one great reason! Moreover, the more you learn about them the more you can provide them with resources they need. That further deepens the relationship and the trust you enjoy.

Now let's spend some time with the word "no." "No" is a powerful word. It prevents many small business owners from attempting sales. They are so afraid that anyone they contact will say "no" that they avoid making calls or doing any kind of outreach. You need to hit this head-on and dispel the monster that is "no."

What does "no" really mean? It really means "not now." It isn't a value judgement about you. The truth is that when someone says "no" to you, they aren't saying something bad about you. They don't even know you! They are merely saying they don't want to explore what you offer right now. Or they aren't in the market *right now*.

That's great news! You should welcome the word "no" because it keeps you from investing a lot of time on something that isn't going to happen. When you're prospecting, and you encounter people who avoid you, you should give them permission to say "no." They're avoiding you because they don't want to be in a confrontation. They're afraid to say "no." So, they go radio silent. If you are prospecting to someone who won't answer or return a phone call, consider leaving them a message like this:

> *"Hi, this is Diane from ABC Company. I thought there might be value in us having a conversation about your (situation that my product/service addresses). Since I haven't heard back from you, I'm thinking something has come up that is of a higher priority right now. No worries! I understand. I'm going to step away for now. I'll put a note in my files to reach out to you again in a couple of months to see if anything has changed. If, in the meantime, you'd like to have that conversation, please call me at 555-555-5555."*

If you've had the sales meeting, and for some reason haven't been able to schedule a follow up meeting you may find it difficult to reconnect with the prospect. This happens quite frequently when the salesperson doesn't gather enough information. In this case, you may want to call and leave a message letting them know you aren't sure what it is they need exactly. In this message you should tell them that if they've decided not to move forward it's really okay. There's no problem with telling you "no" and that you don't want to keep calling them if they don't want to buy the product or service.

When the prospect hears that it's okay to say "no" they are more likely to do so. What a relief! Now you know where they stand, and you can move on.

One aspect of sales to keep in mind is that timing plays a key role. Customers buy when they need or want something, not when you want to sell to them. That's another reason why it's important to continue to build relationships with prospects and current customers. It also speaks to the concept that you can't convince someone to buy from you no matter how eloquent you are! If they avoid you or say "no", consider that you may be contacting them at the wrong time. So, don't let the word "no" trip you up. It's just a word. And it tells you that you can move on.

Moreover, sales is a daily activity. Yet, there's a strange phenomenon around selling that goes like this—the last week of the month is crazy. Salespeople use that time to push offers so they can realize their quotas. Suddenly, deals, discounts, and add-ons are available; anything to entice the buyer to make a decision.

Where were these deals at the beginning of the process? What is the actual value of the product or service? The messaging is, in truth, damaging to your brand and results. Consumers are pretty smart. They quickly figure out that if they hold out until the end of the month, they'll get a better deal. Who doesn't believe that buying a car on the last day of the month will get you the best price? Exactly!

These last minute deals signal to your prospect that you are desperate, and that you think they are an idiot. So much for trust! You are now in a transactional relationship with them.

Your value is limited to the lowest price. Lost is any real value your product/service and company offer. It's a terrible position to be in.

So, don't do it. When you work your process every day you won't be in a bind at the end of the month. You will gain sales consistently over time. And, you will build meaningful, long-term relationships.

Following up is a critical part of lost business. The truth is you are probably going to lose customers here and there. It happens. I didn't believe it when I first became a salesperson. After all I reasoned, as long as we are providing a great product at a great price why would they leave? Well, because other things happen and then they leave.

There is value in knowing why someone stops working with you as it can help you make improvements if necessary. There are also times when it has nothing to do with you, your company, your offering.

In either case there's value in following up with them at some point to see how they are and if things have changed. Don't think they will come back to you if their situation changes. It might happen, and then again, it might not. Determine a length of time that feels reasonable to you and put an appointment on your calendar to give them a call.

Making Inside Sales Work

"Inside Salespeople should engage in the same sort of relationship building activities as outside salespeople – with the exception of attending events."

The first thing to consider with inside sales is what exactly you want your team to do. Do you want them to do outbound calling to set appointments for the outside team? Do you want them to only take incoming calls? Would you like them to upsell current customers? Are you expecting them to make outgoing prospecting calls?

Inside sales can be slightly more challenging than outside sales. The inside sales agent has to be able to develop relationships via phone, skype, zoom, email, etc. They don't have the benefit of being seen at events or in the community so their trust building can be difficult. That's not to say they can't build trust. They can. It just takes a certain skill level that not everyone has.

This is why it's important to have real clarity around what you expect of an inside sales team. We'll explore three different possibilities.

Order Taker

This is not necessarily a "sales" role. This person answers the phone and takes orders from people who have already decided they want to buy something. The Order Taker should be knowledgeable enough about the product or service to be able to ensure the caller gets the right things. Sometimes people think they know what they need when in reality, they don't. It's important that the Order Taker know what questions to ask to develop a clear understanding of the need.

In addition, when the Order Taker is knowledgeable they can identify additional or alternative products or services that might be valuable to the caller. That kind of customer care can make the difference between a one time engagement and repeat business.

Appointment Setters

These are people whose sole responsibility is to call prospects to secure meetings for the outside sales team. I am not a fan of dialing for dollars. I think it's not a productive use of time. Because of that, I believe the Appointment Setter should spend some of their time actually researching the people or companies in the target market. The more they can learn, the more they can connect to when calling to schedule a meeting.

This also allows them the opportunity to winnow the field and call those companies/people with the highest odds of wanting to meet. Appointment setting can be a tricky practice. If the setter is compensated for the number of appointments they set, they can omit the qualification step and just set any appointment they can. That ends up being a waste of the outside salesperson's time.

Some people say "yes" just to get you off the phone. They don't really have any intention of following through with a meeting. That's why it's better to have a process that includes research. Appointment Setters should call people they can have a meaningful conversation with. Their odds of getting the meeting for the outside salesperson will be much higher, AND the meeting will actually take place.

Inside Salesperson

Let's be realistic about this person. The expectation is that they are going to do outbound calling in an attempt to sell to prospects, and to upsell current customers. Since sales requires trust and involves timing and need, an inside sales team should not be expected to spend their time dialing a list of prospects. They shouldn't be expected to read a script that is designed to convince the recipient to buy.

Inside Salespeople should engage in the same sort of relationship building activities as outside salespeople—with the exception of attending events. Inside Salespeople have to rely on their phone and written communication skills.

A great place to build those skills and relationships is with current customers. The Inside Salesperson should spend time checking in with current customers to see how they are doing, what's going on, if they have any new initiatives on the horizon and the like. The Inside Salesperson can connect the customer to resources and vendors. They can send them valuable articles, congratulatory cards when there is an event, milestone, media mention. It's the same relationship building techniques an outside salesperson would use. The Inside Salesperson just isn't going to visit the customer.

When it comes to engaging in outbound prospecting and selling, the Inside Salesperson should follow the same process as an outside salesperson. They should build relationships, research their target market, and engage in outreach that results in meetings. Of course, those meetings will take place via phone or video conference. The sale will come only after the meeting has taken place and the salesperson has been able to do their discovery.

Business owners and sales managers should avoid creating an inside sales team with the sole purpose of dialing for dollars. It doesn't work, AND it can ruin your reputation. You will become known as a telemarketer and everyone will stop answering the phone when you call. So, adopt the same principles used for outside sales. Success will follow.

Marketing Isn't Selling

"Marketing is about awareness, while selling
is about discovery."

Sales and marketing are often lumped together. And it can be confusing deciding where the line is. In simple terms, marketing is about exposure and awareness. Sales is about working with a prospect to explore whether there's an opportunity to provide a solution to a problem.

Marketing and prospecting often overlap. For example, networking can be considered marketing and prospecting. You are building relationships, gaining exposure, getting the opportunity to talk about your company. Networking isn't, however, selling.

Following the premise that marketing is about gaining exposure and awareness for your product or service, you can include public speaking, writing, and podcasting to more traditional activities. Many of us think of print, TV, and radio advertising when we think about marketing. We also think about direct mail, newsletters, and billboards. But, what about social media? Well, it's a valuable avenue for marketing, as long as it's handled appropriately. And this is an area where people blur the lines.

Social media allows you to share your knowledge, your value, your expertise so that others can decide if you have something they'd be interested in. You also have the opportunity to connect with people so you can build meaningful business relationships. Unfortunately, some people use social media to try to sell their product or service to total strangers. That's not what anyone should be doing. We'll talk in more detail about how to use social media for marketing later in this chapter.

For now, let's talk about what selling is. Selling is really about connecting your offering to someone's need. In order to do that, you first have to learn about them and their situation. While marketing is about awareness, selling is about discovery.

Those are two sides of the same coin. When determining where and how to market, decide who you want to build relationships with, who you should be getting in front of, and where your target audience will best hear your message. Remembering that the message is NOT "Buy my stuff." Focus on what you want them to know. How can you position your company so it's attractive to your potential client or colleague? That's the question to be answered. Then execute.

Once you are in a conversation with someone who has interest in learning more about what you have to offer, your first task is to learn about them. Yep, it isn't to go ahead and tell them about your product or service. That's not very effective.

Frankly, they aren't listening to everything you're telling them. Ask them enough questions to get to the core of their situation and their values. Then, and only then, can you determine if you should be pursuing a business relationship with them.

Sales and marketing aren't the same thing and they don't intersect. Think of it as a relay. You market to create awareness about the value of your offering. You discover whether the prospect is really a potential customer through the sales process. When it makes sense, you connect your product/service to their situation.

Okay, now let's talk about social media. Social media is great for marketing, connecting, networking, and doing research. It's NOT the place to sell. There are several ways you can use social media to meet people and build relationships with resources, and potential customers. As with everything else we've explored in this book, your participation on social media should be geared toward learning, sharing, and connecting. You never know who you are engaging with or who they know. You also don't know how you can add value to them, or how they can add value to you, until you know them.

The challenge is determining where you should be participating, how you should be engaging, and what system you should use to ensure consistency.

One thing to embrace about social media marketing is that the best campaigns are informational; sharing information and knowledge works really well with social media. You are positioning your company as the expert in the field. That's how you build trust. So, when you are thinking about creating a strategy, think about what you know that you can share.

Start with what you are hoping to accomplish. All marketing should have a goal. What do you want people to do? Social media does not respond well to 'buy now' types of marketing campaigns. However, you have a great opportunity to create awareness and action that connects you to your buyer.

So, what do you want people to do? Call or visit your business? Clip a coupon? Watch a video? Attend an event? Be very clear and specific about what you want this particular campaign to accomplish. You will have a chance to implement other campaigns in the future. It's important to realize that marketing is the kind of thing that changes over time. As your goals change, your marketing will change with it. So, don't get caught up thinking that you have to have one sensational marketing campaign. Sensational would be great! However, you will want to create and implement marketing campaigns over time. So, focus on the goal at hand.

Now that you know what you want people to do, ask yourself this key question—Which people? What does your target audience look like? And please don't think it's everyone, or everyone with a roof, for example! It isn't. Your best clients have things in common. Use the information you developed through the form in the Resources section of this book. Knowing who you're targeting is instrumental in creating your marketing strategy. You probably have a couple of target audiences. You aren't going to message to all of them in the same way or the same places. For example, if one of your target audiences is over 80 years old, social media marketing may not be the way to go. Traditional marketing is probably more effective with them. If a target market is women in their 40s or 50s, Facebook is ideal.

When your message is broad because you're trying to hit everyone, you'll hit no one. Your message should be specific and should be directed at a clear target audience. This is how they'll hear it. Remember that you can implement other marketing campaigns to reach out to other audiences. Stay away from trying to hit all of them at once. That's a message that will be so big that no one will hear it and you won't accomplish your goal.

Once you know what you want to say, and who you want to say it to, you must decide where you should be communicating. This is a critical part of marketing success.

There's a danger of getting caught up in trying to do what the business next door is doing. Or what someone tells you to do. However, that's not necessarily the best thing for your business! You want to be where your target audience is going to hear your message.

For example, if you are selling to consumers you probably want to have a Facebook business page. That's a great place to connect with people who need your product or service. You might also decide to send a postcard with a coupon or advertise in the local paper or advertising publication. Remember to ask the question: Where does your audience receive information? There are a lot of places online where you can post. Ask yourself where your target is and how do they consume information.

Let's explore some options that you might not be thinking about but have impact:

Video—using video in your social media marketing can have an incredible impact. Video gives you the chance to demonstrate your product, or share a how-to. It also gives your audience a chance to see you. Don't underestimate how powerful this can be. People buy from people they trust. One of the best ways to build trust is to talk to people directly. Video gives you that opportunity. You can post your videos on YouTube and/or Vimeo. Then you can share them on other platforms like Facebook, LinkedIn, or Twitter. You can also use video in blog posts and email marketing. Doing live video on Instagram can be a great way to build a community. There are also sites where you can have your own video channel. The power of the community of marketers drives exposure to everyone. An example is www.EliteExpertsVideoNetwork.com.

Guest Blogging—if there are blogs out there that you follow, start commenting on the posts. Once you've developed a relationship with the blog owner, ask if you can provide a guest article. That can get you in front of their audience which can elevate your credibility and exposure.

Podcasts—there are a lot of podcasts that seek guests to share expertise. Do some research to find the ones that make sense for your business. Then reach out to the host. Remember that this is not a commercial for your business. You share your expertise around some aspect of your industry. You then have a link you can share through your social media platforms. Being a guest on a podcast can increase your credibility. Hosting a podcast is another way to build credibility and a community around your business. You can be the only contributor to the content, or you can bring on guests who you interview or have a conversation with. Podcasting has become very popular and consumers are always looking for great content.

Email marketing—often overlooked, email marketing is one of the most effective marketing methods available today.

Not only does it allow you to stay connected to your audience, but you can now connect your marketing email to your social profiles. This expands the reach of the email. Visit the Resources section of this book for more information and guidelines. You can also track who clicks on which links. This lets you know who is interested in what. You can then tailor your marketing to more narrow audiences.

Online Courses—Why not create a program where you teach someone something they need to know? If you've got the knowledge, there are people out there wanting to learn. And they want to do it on their own terms and time. Online courses are a great way to increase credibility and visibility while also having another income stream.

If you're new to social media marketing pick ONE avenue and get used to it. Consistency is critical to social media marketing success. So don't overdo it right out of the gate. Give yourself the chance to get used to the process and build steam. You can always add to your strategy as you move forward.

Think about where your target audience is going to hear your message, determine what you want them to know and do, and then decide how you want to connect with them. Social media marketing is really about connecting and building trust. That's why it's "social" marketing. As you build awareness around your company you will find that your marketing momentum will build. Your company will become a household name and people will share your information with their networks. The spider web of the internet will expand your efforts and you will realize a significant impact to your business growth.

It's important to keep your "social" professional. For some businesspeople social media can be a little confusing. "Social" in business is not the same as "social" in life. It's important that you understand the difference and how to engage if you want to connect effectively.

While it is true that people do business with people, there's a line you don't want to cross. "Social" doesn't mean talking about any, and every, thing. There is a professional way to be social.

Wherever you choose to interact online you should err on the side of professionalism. This means considering what you're posting, where you're interacting, what you're saying, and what you hope to achieve.

Some social media platforms have opportunities for businesses and people to participate. Take Facebook, for example. You can have a personal profile where you connect with friends and family. You can also have a business page, where you engage with customers and prospects. Both have value. The difference is this—you don't want to talk a lot about business on your personal profile, and you don't want to talk about personal things on your business page.

When you have a meeting with a prospect or a client, how personal do you get? Probably not very, unless you know them very well. That same philosophy and level of professionalism should be used online. Building business relationships is a process. You build them with respect, patience, and curiosity.

Use each platform the way it is meant to be used. LinkedIn is a totally professional site. There is no opportunity to post personal information here. This is a place to build business relationships. Remember, you can communicate privately on any social media platform. When you're publicly posting, respect the platform you are on. Ensure your posts are proper for the audience.

Following this idea that relationship building happens over time, you can use social media platforms to assist you in the process. Once you connect with someone online you can suggest a phone call or short meeting so you can get to know them better. You can share something you find interesting with them and engage in conversation over time.

The question to ask is, "why are you connecting with someone?" The answer should be, "to build a relationship with them." The answer isn't, "to sell them something." Gaining a sale happens once you've earned trust. Trust happens over time. So, if you focus on building the relationship, instead of the sale, you'll not only gain a sale where it makes sense, but you'll probably gain a great referral source.

Ask yourself the question, "What does that other person want to know?" If you engage online with a focus on what matters to others you will surely maintain a proper level of professionalism. Your "social" will be on the right track. The results will be what you are looking for. And the relationships you build will serve your business over time.

Tradeshows can be a great way to connect with clients, prospects and referral partners. It's good to be seen and to see what's out there. However, if not handled well, a tradeshow can be an expensive waste of time. So, what can you do to improve your odds of success? Have a plan and work the plan.

The first step in tradeshow success is knowing why you're there. What do you hope to achieve? Are you hoping to do some prospecting? Would you like to make some connections with possible referral partners? Maybe you're look to grow your contact base and gain more newsletter readers. Whatever the reason, define it clearly. This will help you develop your plan for how you'll handle your booth and the follow up after the show.

One aspect of tradeshow involvement that often goes unrealized is the pre-work. This is where you make sure you let people know that you'll be exhibiting. Create an outreach plan to inform your prospects, clients, and associates of your booth. Give them a reason to stop by, like a giveaway or information on a new product or service. Your goal is to drive traffic to your booth. You want people seeking you out.

The next part is to plan the format of the booth. What will your message be? This depends on who you are trying to attract. Like any marketing, you want your booth to be attractive to your target. How will you engage with the people who stop by your booth? What do you want them to walk away with? This is best determined early on. That way you can be sure you have everything you need at your booth on the day of the show.

For example, if you want to gather newsletter readers you need to have a way to capture people's email addresses. You can have a sign-up sheet or a fishbowl for business cards. If you want to identify potential prospects you might want to have a giveaway form where they answer a couple of qualifying questions. This form is used to determine a winner of the giveaway and provides you with great information.

If you're demonstrating a new product or service, you might want to have a looping video playing at the booth. This is useful for providing information to visitors while you're talking with someone else. And while we're on the subject of talking to visitors, be sure you have your 30-second introduction down pat. I suggest adding a question you can ask the visitor to quickly determine whether they're truly interested in your product or whether they're there for the giveaway. You don't want to spend your time talking with the people who stopped by just to get the pen, mousepad, or other free giveaway trinket.

This, of course, speaks to understanding why people visit booths in the first place. As I mentioned, some come only for the trinkets. Others come with a real need for the product or service. They're taking this opportunity to gather as much information as they can.

A reason you may not realize is the approachability of the booth staff. If the people staffing the booth are sitting behind the table talking to each other, or checking their email on their smartphone, or talking with another booth attendant, visitors will walk right by. They want to feel welcomed; they want to know you want to talk with them. This doesn't mean that you have to be aggressive or obnoxious. A friendly demeanor wins the day. Look people in the eye with a smile on your face and say hello, or good morning. Stand in front of the table, not behind it. And don't sit unless there are no attendees walking around.

When a tradeshow is paired with an educational event there'll be times that attendees will be in classes or seminars. At those times, the traffic on the tradeshow floor is very light.

That's a good time to visit other booths, check your email, or sit down. Otherwise, it's marketing and you are on!

Lastly, determine how you are going to follow up with the people you meet. This is an area where a lot of people fall down. They get back to the office after a couple of days at a tradeshow and they fail to follow up in a timely fashion. It begs the question—why even have a booth if you aren't going to follow up?

Ideally, you want to follow up with the qualified prospects and potential referral partners within one week of the end of the last day of the show. Keep the momentum going; don't let the trail go cold. You want to connect while the whole event is still top of mind so that you don't find yourself reminding the other person who you are and where you're from.

One way to plan for follow up is to have a hook, something that visitors can sign up for. When I shared a booth at a show with other coaches, we offered 1 hour of free coaching to those people who put their business card in a bowl. There were three bowls designated for 3 different types of coaching. After the show, we divvied up the cards and reached out to those visitors. That's just one example of what you can do. Remember the form I mentioned earlier? That form gives you information on who is interested in hearing from you after the show. Make sure you follow up with those people.

Planning for your tradeshow experience is the best way to ensure your success. Securing a booth at a tradeshow can cost time and money. You want to get the most out of it. So, identify why you're exhibiting, what you hope to achieve, how you'll engage and follow up. You'll find it more worthwhile.

Account Maintenance

"Ask yourself how well you know your customers."

Nurturing and maintaining current client relationships is one of the best ways to grow your business. It takes a plan and commitment. Think about it. when you sell something, what do you do next? Do you have a process for staying in touch with your customer? Even when you have recurring sales, there is still value in setting time aside to have conversations with your clients. The recurring business is a transaction. The conversations are relationship building.

We all know how important it is to follow up with a client after you do the work. The question is how to do it well. The first thing I'm going to say is this—don't follow up via email. Follow up with a phone call. The client matters to you. The work you do matters to you. Don't leave the follow up to misinterpretation or getting lost in the massive amount of emails people get.

Unless a client prefers email as the means of communication, do yourself a favor and call them on the phone. You want them to hear your tone of voice, your confidence. An email can't do that for you. In addition, if there was a problem, you want to be able to address it immediately. I'm not sure you can do that through email as effectively as via phone.

The second thing I'm going to say is the sooner the better. I think you should check in within a week of the order; ideally within 2 days. If you want to be sure everything went well, be sure as soon as possible. That way if something went wrong, you're on it. It shows caring and strength.

When you do call, what do you say? There's the fear you'll sound like you aren't sure whether you delivered a quality product. Or that you are fearful something went wrong. You think that you want to show confidence in your work but if you call to check in it will somehow be interpreted as insecurity.

I believe it's critically important to communicate with your clients before, during and after the sale. You can pre-empt any discomfort by letting your clients know your process—and that the follow up call is simply part of it. That way they will expect it and won't think twice about why you are calling.

Your clients want to know that you care. They want to know you aren't just in it for the sale; you're in it for the long haul. And that means you're going to be sure everything went according to plan. Things happen; life can get in the way. It's not unusual and I think most people respect that sometimes circumstances beyond your control can impact the job you do. Don't you want to know as quickly as possible whether there was a hiccup? That way you can deal with it head on. In addition, the follow up call gives you the opportunity to communicate with the client one more time. You can use this opportunity to deepen the relationship, and possibly find out about the next need.

Imagine if you didn't follow up on a project. You either assumed everything went according to plan, or you were uncomfortable calling to check. And now imagine that something **did** go wrong. The client knows it because they've experienced it. You, however, have no idea. And because you aren't calling to follow up, you won't find out until you try to sell them something else. When they don't take your call, you're in trouble!

So, while this may feel uncomfortable, it is, in my opinion, a critical step in the sales process. It is also a place where words matter. You can phrase the follow up call in a way that lets your client know exactly where you're coming from. You can let them know that you gave the account your all and are confident everything went well. AND that you know that sometimes things happen that are out of your control. Because they matter to you, you want to be sure they are completely happy with the end product.

Here's a couple of examples of phrasing that works:

Vendor: "Our standard procedure is to produce the product, ship it, and give you a call within the week to confirm everything was to your liking."

Vendor on the follow up call: "Hi it's Diane. Just checking in as promised. The product is great, isn't it?"

Now this is a very confident tone and may be uncomfortable for some people. It really depends on how you say these words.

You can laugh as you say them so there's levity. You can ask it as a serious question. You can say it strongly.

Vendor on the follow up call: "Hi, it's Diane. Just checking in on the job we just finished for you. From our end, it couldn't have been better. Because your business is very important to us, we want to be sure everything went as you expected."

Vendor on the follow up call with a regular client: "Hi, it's Diane. Just making sure this job went as well as all the previous jobs and that you are thrilled! We never want to assume success, even when everything looks perfect."

Do you see what I'm doing? I'm letting them know I'm confident that we did a great job **and** asking if they feel the same way. I'm letting them know I care about them and the work we do for them. I'm not hiding, hoping they won't call. I'm hitting it head-on. Most likely they have a policy within their company to check with their clients, so following up won't seem odd.

When you care enough to do the best job you can, you care enough to make sure the client is completely happy with the results. You're confident in your work, so you're confident enough to ask the question. You'll be respected for it and the client will really know that you care about their business.

It's just as important to have a mechanism to make sure the customer is receiving consistent, quality attention. Whether the salesperson is given responsibility for maintaining this relationship or not, he/she should still have a system for checking in with his/her clients.

We have a lot of opportunities to connect with our customers and yet, it seems we do it less. And then we're surprised when we lose their business. Or we wonder why we struggle to get more business from them. There's a lot of ways we can continue to nurture client relationships.

First, continue to be interested in them, in how their business is. If you sell to consumers, continue to be curious about them and their lives. After all, you were interested in them when you were trying to win their business, so stay interested after the sale!

Set up a structure or system; something you can do in an automated way. For example, text when you have something going on. An e-newsletter is great when you have information you want to share. But that's not enough. You want to set up a system on a consistent basis to make sure you know what's going on with them. It's not about you. It's about them, what they need, where they're going, what they're moving toward.

One word of caution—if you provide an ongoing service to your customers, don't use that service as your touchpoints. It doesn't count because that's what they pay you for. There's a difference between being connected to a customer because you provide them a product or service, and being connected because you want to know how they are.

Ask yourself how well you know your customers. How much do you know about them, their goals, and their challenges? If you work with mid-size and large companies, how many people do you have a connection to? One of the worst things that can happen is to be in a relationship with only one person and then that person leaves.

Some examples of account management activities are: Schedule short meetings with your client to find out how they are. No sales agenda. Just find out how they're doing. When you're networking you develop relationships with companies that have products and services that could be valuable to your clients. When you go on a discovery mission to find out what's going on with them, you can offer your resources to them. What better way to show you care!

Schedule a lunch and learn where you bring in a subject matter expert in an area of value to your customer, but that is not what you offer. Invite your customers.

Invite a customer to an event you're going to. When it's a seminar or workshop that could be of value to them, you're providing them with an opportunity to learn something that can help them in their business.

Send the client links or articles on subjects of value to them. It shows you are thinking about them, what matters to them, and what they might need to know.

Sales Managers

*"Establishing a clear, effective policy will
do wonders for everyone!"*

There's a sales management philosophy in too many companies that's actually working against sales growth. And the salespeople know it.

The philosophy goes like this:

- Walk in 40 doors a day
- Make 40 calls a day
- Hand your business card to everyone
- Gather as many business cards as you can
- Sell, Sell, Sell

While this is a lot of activity and can look good on a sales report, it isn't usually productive. It shifts the goal from getting business, to participating in a specific behavior. It might have worked for the sales manager when he/she was a salesperson. That doesn't mean it'll work for other people.

Many companies with this philosophy have a lot of turnover in their sales department. And do you know why? It's because people join the company with the best of intentions and in many cases a great method for gaining sales. When they discover they can't implement their method but rather, have to engage in behavior that doesn't work for them, they don't hit their sales goals. So, they leave—either voluntarily or by request. Either way, it's not good for the company. The cost of just having to bring on one new employee is significant.

There's value in doing the math. Take your cost of advertising for candidates, cost of interviewing, onboarding, training, and exiting employees. Multiply the total by the number of salespeople who have come and gone in the sales department over the past year. Now add in the soft cost of unrealized sales. This number is a ballpark of what you were expecting the person to bring in during that year. What would it do for your company to reduce those expenses AND gain those revenues?

If your company is struggling to achieve sales growth and has salespeople coming and going, you might want to take a look at your policies and expectations. When you accept the premise that the more you think about selling the less you will sell, you realize that the philosophy outlined above is totally focused on selling. So, no wonder it doesn't work!

Not to mention the image that develops of the company in the community. Stop for a minute and think about how your company may be perceived by your prospect base. If you have a revolving door outside your sales department, your prospects are continuously experiencing someone new trying to sell to them. That sort of instability does not instill confidence and trust. Prospects are right to wonder what you care most about.

Take a step back and ask yourself what matters most. Is it gaining sales or engaging in specific activities? You know my vote! Gaining more sales. Now, ask yourself why you hired any of your salespeople. What was it about them that you liked? If you hired them because you thought they would be good at bringing in business, then let them go do that! If you hired them for their list of previous clients, be careful. Just because they gained that list in the past doesn't mean they'll be able to bring them along. They may not have developed a good relationship with those clients.

A good sales manager knows they'll be successful when their salespeople are successful. It's not about what worked for the manager; it's about what works for the sales staff—individually. Respecting their unique capabilities and needs will help each person as well as the team.

A good sales manager knows their salespeople. They've taken time to get to know them and how they operate. They've talked with them about how they plan to succeed, and what they need to make that happen. Then the sales manager works with the salesperson to help them craft a plan that is unique to them. Together they develop a reporting system that makes sense.

It's the sales manager's job to work with their salespeople in a way that is best for them, not the manager themselves. This individualized attention will ensure that each salesperson's needs are being met and that they have the tools they need to succeed. Since no two people are the same, it stands to reason that no two people will require the same plan and assistance to reach their goals.

Creating a one-size fits all type of sales program only works for the sales manager. It makes it easier on them because they will expend less effort when working with the team. Unfortunately, it isn't going to get them the results that they want.

In addition, sales managers need to allow their salespeople to build relationships with people who may or may not need what they have to sell. The best thing a salesperson can do is spend their time building relationships with other business professionals who can help him/her gain access to ideal prospects. What is better than a referral? Not much!

That doesn't mean the salesperson won't have to do some sort of cold outreach. They will. It's simply true that good relationships lead to more business over time.

As the small business owner, if you aren't doing the sales then you are the sales manager. Think about the brand you're establishing. Brand is not what you say it is; it's how your company is experienced and perceived in the marketplace. You want to be sure your salespeople support your brand when they are engaging with others. Remember, you're in this for the long term. How you "manage" your sales team, and how they show up in the community, have direct impact on how successful you'll be.

Having a sales department policy is the foundation of success for any organization, no matter how big or small. Whether you have one, or one hundred salespeople, you need to have clearly defined guidelines and expectations. This keeps everyone on the same course and provides metrics for measuring results.

Establishing a clear, effective policy will do wonders for everyone! Setting clear expectations with attached consequences provides a baseline; something to refer to as the blueprint.

The vision and goals of the organization are the starting point for all departmental policies. They're especially important to the sales team because it's these people who are going to be the face of your company to the outside world. They must understand who you are.

The what, who, and where are critical. What do you sell? This is the section where you talk about the actual product or service. Your sales team needs to have a complete grasp of what it is they're selling. You can insert manuals, sale sheets, and brochures here if they will help your salespeople understand the product or service.

Who is your client? You should have a clear picture of what makes a good client, and conversely, who is not a good client. You don't want your sales team pursuing prospects who aren't really qualified. By sharing with them what an ideal client looks like you help them target their sales efforts.

Where can they sell? Do you have territories? If so, how are they designated? What happens if a salesperson gets a lead for a client in someone else's territory? If you don't have territories are there geographical boundaries? Or do you want your salespeople focusing on a particular size of company or industry? Spell it out.

When it comes to values, methods, and procedures, do you have particular methods you prefer your sales staff use? Do you offer platforms like webinars they can conduct? Do you exhibit at, or attend, tradeshows? Do you have a way for call-ins to be distributed?

Get the point? You don't want to stifle a salesperson by making them sell in a certain way. However, if there are resources and tools you offer to your sales team, put them in writing. If there are certain things you don't want your sales staff doing, like spamming people, tell them that. Make sure everyone knows what they can and cannot do. Then, help them create their own process.

Clarity and consistency make a big difference here. You can't over-communicate. Think about these things from the perspective of someone just walking into the company. They don't know what you know. It can be hard to remember things that you learned at the beginning. However, that's the stuff that your staff needs to know. Your job is to make sure they have all the information they need to be successful.

Let's start with product knowledge. This is where you make sure your staff knows how they'll become familiar with the product or service. Do they go to training? Is there information available online? What materials are available to them? Who is available to answer their questions?

Equally important is this—what is the company's expectation of how long it should take someone to learn about the product or service so that they are capable of selling it? When new items are introduced, how will they be shared with the sales staff?

Along the same lines is explaining what resources are available to the sales team. They need to know who they can turn to for answers. Will they be given a mentor? Will someone ride along with them on sales calls for a period of time? How much autonomy do they have to make decisions about how they quote a prospect? Are there templates?

Compensation is, of course, a huge part of a sales team policy. Not only should you put the compensation plan in writing but also it should be clear, and easy to follow. Anyone should be able to know, at any time, how they're doing. I've seen companies create compensation policies that were so complicated they needed a programmed excel file to determine payment. The result? A lack of trust. The salespeople never really knew if they were being accurately compensated.

In addition, refrain from changing the compensation system too frequently. Determine what makes sense, put it in writing, and stick to it. And, please, make sure it's fair. If you set your staff up for success, they'll exceed your expectations. If you create a structure that's difficult to reach, they'll become frustrated and probably leave. Then all that training and time you've invested in them will be lost.

Along with compensation and performance reviews, there should be performance expectations. What are the sales goals? How will they be evaluated? The goals are tied to compensation so they must be clearly spelled out. Remember to indicate the expectations of new employees versus seasoned.

Performance reviews are also a key aspect of an effective sales team policy. When and how will they be reviewed? What are the criteria upon which they will be evaluated? Make sure you put it in writing and adhere to it. All too often employees go too long without being reviewed. Then something happens and their manager reacts. It's not a good situation.

When you want your sales team to be successful you have to give them timely feedback on how they are doing. Timely feedback means in real time. A sales manager's time is best spent working with her team individually and together. Make sure you indicate in the policy the steps that will be taken to help them improve if necessary. Also include the rewards they'll receive when they meet or exceed your expectations.

Lastly, be sure to let them know if there are opportunities for growth within the organization. If there are, indicate how someone positions themselves for growth. How will they be evaluated, and what can they do to ensure they get those opportunities?

Now let's talk about some best practices. There really are things you can do to make sure you are presenting the best policy for the best results. Some of them we've already touched on. The first and in my opinion guiding principle is to make it success oriented.

Write your sales team policy from a standpoint of wanting everyone to be successful. Talk about what it takes to be successful and how the organization works with the team to ensure that success.

As I said before, make sure it's clear. There's no need for complicated, lengthy prose. Say it straight, so it's understood. Be clear. That's your goal!

Having said that, make sure it's content rich. Say everything you need to say. Don't leave anything out. Lack of information can cause unnecessary problems.

When I talked about compensation, I mentioned to keep it simple. Keep it straightforward and clear. This stance goes along with being success oriented and trustworthy. This is a place where simple and less complicated truly matters. A grade school kid who can add, subtract and multiply should be able to figure it out.

Indicate how you train your staff. I'm talking about product training and professional development training. Do you offer sales training? Or presentations training? How about leadership training to those people who wish to grow with the company? Whatever training you offer, spell it out. What are the guidelines, expectations, and time frames? How do you monitor to make sure the training is working?

My favorite part of the policy is expectations and consequences; mostly because for some reason people avoid this. The truth is you all have expectations around your employee's performance and success. And in reality, there are (or should be) consequences when those expectations are met or not. When you don't communicate them clearly, you create a vague situation that isn't good for anyone.

I submit it is mostly bad for the people who are meeting your expectations to have to put up with people who are not consistently meeting expectations without consequences. This causes dissension and creates a bad environment for everyone. So do unreasonable expectations and consequences. So, keep them reasonable. Remember, you want to set people up for success.

You want the expectations and consequences to be clear and consistent. They have to be the same for everyone. Consider them carefully and then commit them to paper. The best way to avoid 'difficult' conversations is to set the expectation and then follow through with it. When people see that you mean it, they will either perform or leave. And there's a bonus effect—those who are good producers will be happier and bring greater results. When you follow your policies you are telling your producers that you value them. Believe me, they are paying attention.

And equally important is to identify the monitoring system. How will you monitor each person to be sure they are meeting your expectations? That should be included in the policy. Nothing should be left out. You want everyone to know what is expected of them, what they'll gain when they meet or exceed those expectations, and what they'll encounter if they don't. You also want them to know what to expect in terms of how they will be monitored and evaluated.

Clear and consistent communication keeps them from guessing or drawing their own conclusions. It also prevents anyone from being able to say that they didn't know.

This leads us to communication channels. When it comes to communication, consider all the ways people communicate—direction (who to and from), methods (email, phone, reports), dos and don'ts.

How does the leadership communicate with the sales staff, and conversely, how does the sales staff communicate up the chain? Are there reports they're supposed to submit? How often will they report, and with what information? How will leadership acknowledge and respond? What about situations when the salesperson needs assistance or has a question? In other words, those times outside of the reporting cycle.

How are the salespeople expected to communicate with other departments? Are there forms or protocols that are supposed to be followed? Be careful when setting expectations for prospecting. This is where process should be left to the individual salesperson.

What kind of follow up do you expect your salespeople to do with current clients? Some organizations have the salespeople hand off their new clients to inside customer service reps. In this situation the salespeople have no continuing contact with their clients. Other organizations expect their salespeople to maintain relationships with their clients. Whatever you choose, put it in writing.

Before you decide, think about long term consequences. If the salesperson is no longer in contact with the client, how will the company gain more business from them or renew contracts?

Now let's talk about some legal considerations. Whenever you put a policy together and put it in writing you want to be sure that you are following guidelines that will keep you out of trouble. The first is equal employment. Your policies have to be the same for everyone. No playing favorites or having different rules for different people. And I'm not just talking about gender, race, and the like. I'm talking about top performers versus others, family members vs non-family members.

You want to follow guidelines for vehicle use and expense reimbursement. Of course, the pay schedule and guidelines must follow legal practices. There should be a non-compete and a non-disclosure form signed by all sales staff and the information about them should be in the policy. Explain why you have them and what your expectations are.

Identify the work schedule and keep it reasonable. In other words, unless there is a true business reason for the sales team to be in the office at 4pm on a Friday, don't make it part of the schedule. You want your salespeople out making sales and building relationships. Having them come in at 4pm on Friday is really just a way of telling them you don't trust them. As long as they are gaining sales, and are reporting accurately, do you really care where they are? If you do, why do you? Understanding your own beliefs and expectations will help you ensure you're setting reasonable expectations.

And to help make sure you are following federal and local laws, visit the department of labor online and your state government websites.

Knowledge is power. When you create an effective sales team policy that speaks to the company's and the employee's needs you empower everyone to succeed. As you've seen, expectations and consequences are key parts of any effective policy. And remember, you can't over communicate!

One thing I'd steer clear of is engaging in role playing during team meetings. It's a tremendously uncomfortable process for a salesperson and doesn't achieve the goal. If you want to know what a salesperson is saying during a sales call, go with them on a few visits. Have a discussion during a team meeting about best practices. In this way, the team is sharing what they do that works. You can also engage in a conversation around what is challenging. This is a much better way to get the team to provide each other with feedback and input.

In addition, there is great value in creating a feedback loop so your salespeople are coming to you with their questions and challenges. There are times when this conversation is more effective one on one. People don't like to feel like they are being put on the spot. Calling someone out at a meeting only serves to make them nervous and uncomfortable. I submit you will not gain greater insight into what they know, how they interact, or what they say when you engage in this process.

Another thing that works is to break the team up into roundtables. Pick a topic for each table and let the people at the table discuss the topic. They can rotate between tables so all topics are covered.

When the goal is to ensure your team has the knowledge, skill, and resources necessary to be successful you will choose processes that work toward that end. Just remember that making them uncomfortable doesn't work. Not to mention how uncomfortable it makes everyone else in the room! So, avoid the impulse to do things that sound easy. Ask yourself how you would respond or feel. Always consider the goal when making any decisions that impact your team. Setting them up for success should always be your main goal. Keep that in mind, remember they are each unique in how they work, and seek to support them in the way that works for each of them.

Direct Sellers

"The truth is this – friends and family
are not target markets."

There are many opportunities to create a business for yourself. A lot of people choose to sell something they use, believe in and think others will want. I'm talking about direct sales—things like skin care, cosmetics, kitchen utensils, jewelry, and the like.

There's a misconception that the best way to grow this type of business is to reach out to family and friends. After all, they are the people who support you and want you to be successful. Why wouldn't they want to buy from you? Well, because they don't need or want what you are selling.

The truth is this—friends and family are not target markets. They are your support system. However, if you try to sell to them, that will end quickly and uncomfortably. When you pitch your product or service to your family and friends you put them in an awkward position. They don't want to hurt your feelings. And most of the time, they don't want to buy what you're selling. So, what do they do? They might start avoiding you. They might lie to you. Some will tell you the truth. Most, if not all, will be annoyed that you put them in that position. AND, you will not grow your business.

If they aren't the target, who is? Well, probably other people like you. Selling to individuals can be tricky. They don't like being solicited in their homes and marketing only goes so far.

One of the best methods is to engage in information sharing. Schedule workshops or programs where you are teaching people something relevant to the product or service you sell. Be careful to keep it educational. It's a process. When you start with education you can gauge who has interest in learning more. Have a mechanism for capturing that information. Capture tools that work include a signup sheet for email marketing, a short survey handed out at the end of the workshop or seminar asking about future interests, or a short form allowing attendees to check boxes about things they're interested in. Then take the next step only with the people who expressed interest in learning more.

Being detached from the outcome allows you to be totally present in the moment. In other words, when you are providing the educational program your only focus is on providing information. It's not on selling anything. Being focused helps you engage and connect with the attendees. This genuine interest in sharing information with no ulterior motive is what will start the development of relationships.

Remember, people buy from people they trust. No one will trust you if they think you're trying to coerce or fool them into buying from you. They won't trust you if they think you're only providing information so you can sell them something. Educate for education's sake. Period. Allow the relationship to take form naturally. You'll end up selling to the people who really do want your product or service. They'll continue to buy from you over time and will refer you to others.

Let's get more specific about what a process would look like. The first thing to do is identify a target market. As I've mentioned previously in this book, there can be more than one target market. Pick one to focus on. Trying to prospect to too many will dilute your message and your efforts. Use that target market to create a contact list.

Next, schedule a workshop and invite the people on your list. Keep it under 2 hours and have light refreshments. Keep the focus on teaching them something they can take away and implement. Have a data capture process like a sign-up form for email marketing and/or a free short consultation.

After the event, follow up with everyone. Send a thank you for attending to those who didn't sign up for anything. Add to your email list those who did sign up. Schedule free short consults with those who requested them. Shoot an email to those who rsvp'd but didn't come letting them know you missed them and asking if they'd like to be informed of the next event.

For those who requested a free short consultation, ask questions first to uncover their needs, interests, questions. Really listen to what they tell you and only respond to what you hear. Don't try to sell them things they don't need or want. Offer products or services that speak to what you learned.

Follow up is equally important. Continue to interact with those who are now clients. Make sure they are having a good experience. Send email marketing on a consistent basis to current clients and those who've signed up to receive email. This is marketing, not selling. Remember, marketing is about awareness and credibility. In order to successfully build a relationship with prospects you use marketing to share information they find valuable and relevant. Then you are top of mind when they need what you offer. What they don't want is to receive emails trying to sell them something.

And lastly, repeat this process. Set up a consistent schedule of workshops or lunch and learns so you're perpetually adding prospects and clients to your base.

The same is true when you are looking for people to join your team. Let go of the idea that the people you know also want to own a business. Building your team is not about convincing people about the great opportunity in front of them. It is about finding and connecting with people like you; people who value the product or service. People who want to gain income.

Consider the characteristics of a direct seller. Who are they? Are they stay-at-home moms, college students, retirees? Are they someone who has a full-time job and wants some added income?

Once you have a picture of who they are, you can develop a marketing plan to get in front of them. This is another place where having an event like a workshop or seminar can be very effective. Direct outreach will be tricky here because you might have an idea of who could be interested in exploring the opportunity but not necessarily certain people in particular.

Reaching out to your connections can be a great place to start—not to ask them to join your team but to ask them if they know anyone who might want to attend your event. Remember, you are having the event to educate—period. Allowing people the time to decide if they want to join you is the best approach. If you conduct the event with a push to add team members then you will alienate the people you're trying to attract.

Think about where your target audiences gather or receive information. Moms often belong to PTAs. College students have discussion boards. Libraries and coffee shops usually have message boards where you can add a flyer.

Using a program like Meetup.com can be a tremendous value here. Search the site for Meetups near you where your targets are congregating. See if you can attend—not to sell but to connect. Sales begins with relationships. Get to know people so you can identify who might be interested in exploring your opportunity. It might not be the person you meet. It might be someone they know.

The other thing you can do with Meetup.com is create one of your own. This is a way to get in front of people who are looking for a topic like yours. Go through the process of scheduling the event. Then add it to your Meetup. Share it with your network and on social media. Meetup will help you get the word out.

You can also take advantage of Alignable (www.alignable. com). This is a site where you can connect with other businesses in your area. You can add events to the site and share them with your network on the site.

When it comes to adding team members, marketing is where you will expend the greatest effort. You're really trying to get in front of people you don't yet know, to first learn about them, build the relationship, and then if it makes sense, share the opportunity.

Before you engage in any outreach or discussion with ANYONE about your product or service, put yourself in their shoes. Ask yourself how you would feel or react if someone approached you the way you are about to approach them. Only do the things you would be okay with. If you'd be uncomfortable, annoyed or bothered by a behavior, don't do it to others! When you're networking, don't assume that the person you're talking to wants to buy your product or become a team member. They may look like the perfect prospect but looks can be deceiving. Focus on getting to know them, not trying to sell to them.

Direct selling is the same as every other type of selling. It's not about you and it's not about convincing people they need what you have to sell. It's about building relationships and engaging in discovery. Seek to learn about others. It's easier and more effective. When you focus on others, you're more genuine and more relatable. People will want to get to know you and connect you with potential clients/team members.

And remember, growing a business takes time. It's up to you how you spend that time. If you spend it trying to sell in the traditional way—convincing, persuading, asking family and friends—you're going to be in for a long, painful process. If, however, you choose to focus on the relationship building aspect, you'll find you enjoy the process and will build a solid business.

Service Providers

---

*"Changing your mindset can change how
you approach the sales process."*

It can feel challenging to sell a service. After all, a service isn't something someone can touch. Connecting and establishing credibility is critical when selling a service. And while it can be somewhat easier to prospect when selling to businesses as opposed to individuals, the premise remains the same. You can't sell anything to anyone. You can, however, build relationships and solve problems with your service.

So, where do you begin? How can you engage in business development in ways that are effective? Start by letting go of the focus on growing your business. Instead, focus on what value you can bring to others; what you have that others need. Why do they need it? What will it do for them or their business? Now, how can you start the process of connecting? If you sell to businesses, consider these ideas:

Schedule and host weekly "live" events online. Offering some insights around a topic of value to your target market on a consistent basis through live video gives them a chance to get to know you in a safe way. These don't have to be lengthy; the shorter the better. Pre-plan your topics, schedule the day of the week and time of day, and spread the word. Then be patient while you grow an audience. Include a way to ask a question related to the topic so you can continue the engagement with your audience in a different format. It could be that you email them an answer directly. Now you're in a one-on-one conversation with them. Or you can text an answer or offer to answer during your next live event.

Offer to conduct a seminar for your client, or resource's, top clients. Tell your client, or your referral partner, that you're happy to give a seminar to their preferred clients free of charge. They get to offer it as a client appreciation program to their most valued clients, and you get to provide valuable information. This can be a great way to get in front of potential clients. After all, the companies trust the host, and so they will trust you. You're bridging the trust gap while starting the process of providing value. It doesn't cost you anything. It does help your relationship with that client or resource. After all, you're providing them with a way to give back to their best customers. Everybody wins.

If you sell to individuals the same rules apply. You want to create ways you can answer their questions, educate them, and build relationships without selling. No ulterior motives! Just focus on them. One possibility is to create a program where you expose them to a variety of resources they may need. Yours is then one of many, but you're the host. Now you're doing something for prospective customers as well as other solution providers.

The more information you share the more trust you build. Remember there are 3 types of people: The **Do Nothings**, the **DIYers**, and the **Prospects**. When you share your knowledge you are sharing to all three groups. What matters is how they respond.

The **Do Nothings** will do nothing with the information you share. That's because they do nothing. They won't try to do things themselves and they won't hire you. So, in truth, they don't really matter.

The **DIYers** will absorb what you share and then do the work themselves. They like to do things themselves. That's okay. They will value you for sharing and will probably refer you to people who don't like to do things themselves.

The **Prospects** are the most important group. They are who you should be talking to at all times. While they may be able to do things themselves, they don't want to. They want to engage with trusted providers. Giving away your knowledge is a great way to be that person. The **Prospect** realizes that you know what you're talking about and trusts you to help them.

So many service providers tell me that sales just isn't their strong suit. I think what they're saying is that they're uncomfortable with the whole idea of selling. I don't have a problem with that because I think they're imagining that they have to sell the old way.

Changing your mindset can change how you approach the sales process. You can be more effective, happier and successful, engaging in a process that is built around curiosity and discovery rather than telling, persuading, and convincing.

These are just a handful of ideas. The point is to think about how you can be a giver to prospective customers, current clients, resources, and potential referral partners. If you can become the go-to for clients and colleagues, you'll grow your business and your reputation.

Retail Sales

*"Successful retail sales has a lot to do
with customer experience."*

Retail has its own set of sales challenges. Your marketing gets people in the door. And it provides you with vehicles for consistent exposure to customers and prospects. However, selling really only happens when they enter your establishment, or visit your website.

Retail sales follow the same guidelines and mindset as any other kind of sales. The focus should be on the prospect or customer. When you think about your own shopping experiences you probably have good, and bad, memories.

Is there really a better way to engage with retail customers? Yes, there really is. Start with why—why does someone come into your store? To shop? To explore? To find something they need? To find a gift for someone else?

What do you know about them? If they're not a repeat customer, you don't know anything about them. Now is a perfect time to start the relationship building process. The first thing you don't know is whether they'd like some assistance or would rather be left alone to browse.

So, how about a simple welcome. Something like this, "Hi. Thanks for stopping in. I'm here if you need any help or can answer any questions you may have." From that point, follow their lead. And make sure you really are available—without lurking. If they ask for assistance, all of the basic sales principles kick in. Listen attentively to what they tell you. Ask enough questions to really learn what they need/want. Then, when you have something that matches what you heard, show them. Don't try to upsell them or offer products before you know what they want. Don't think about what you want to sell them. As with any other selling situation, it's about the customer.

Successful retail sales has a lot to do with customer experience. The more the person enjoys the environment and feels valued, the more likely they are to buy, recommend, and return in the future.

Experience includes things like the appearance of the shop, the behavior of the staff, and availability of products. The environment should be clean, organized, and inviting. It may sound obvious, but there are many establishments not paying attention to what they look and feel like to their patrons. Possibly more important is the behavior of the staff. It's one thing to give someone space to explore. It's another to make them feel like they are imposing. All staff members should present a happy, non-pushy, helpful posture. They shouldn't be so engaged in conversation that they ignore customers. Moreover, they shouldn't share their displeasure with customers, co-workers, etc with the patrons.

That clean and organized environment should include a plentiful display of products. Make it easy for customers to find what they're looking for. And if they need help, do so happily. This is something that is also important when people are shopping on your website. If they need customer service, that experience can be the difference between gaining a customer or a bad review.

No one wants to buy from an establishment that feels dim; where the staff is disinterested or unpleasant; where they feel pressured to buy. Think about what you'd want people to say about their experience in your shop and then ensure you are providing that level of engagement every day.

Franchisors and Franchisees

---

*"Many people who buy a franchise spend their
life savings in the acquisition."*

Everything we've talked about in this book applies to the
franchise world as well. Franchisors try diligently to sell
franchises to people they believe will be successful. And they
provide a degree of sales training. Unfortunately, there are times
when this training is insufficient or misguided.

Franchisees need to embrace the truths of sales outlined
in this book. Their time is best spent being in the community,
building relationships with people, and being of help. Gone are
the days of walking in 40 doors or making 40 phone calls. It just
doesn't work. The landscape is very competitive and consumers
(both individuals and companies) are interested in doing business
with people they trust. They aren't going to buy from you simply
because you walk in their door, interrupt their business or life,
and try to convince them they need what you sell.

The franchisor can help their franchisees succeed by either providing them internal sales training that focuses on discovery instead of selling, or by adding sales training to their franchise fees and enlisting the services of a sales training company that can teach them discovery.

If we focus on goals, the franchisor's goal is to have a large percentage of successful owners. That's how they receive and maintain high ratings and are able to attract new franchisees. It's also how they make money consistently over time. With this as the goal, the franchisor has a vested interest in helping their franchisees succeed.

It seems the franchise world has fallen into the same trap that large corporations fell into. It's the belief that activity leads to sales. That belief is paired to the idea that a process that worked for someone years ago will work for everyone now. First of all, there is no one best way to sell. Each person has to develop a process that works best for them. Just because my process works for me doesn't mean it'll work for you. In addition, methods that might have worked 20—30 years ago just won't work now.

No one wants to be 'sold' anything. We avoid salespeople. We don't answer our phones. We delete unsolicited emails from strangers. And we don't want to be interrupted by a drop in. This all adds up to wanting to be respected.

The franchisee's goal is to succeed in the business they've invested in. Many people who buy a franchise spend their life savings in the acquisition. They need to be able to sell effectively. The best way to support them is to help them build a sales process that can be comfortably conducted, monitored, and repeated over time.

Acknowledgment & Gratitude

"Feeling and expressing gratitude is a huge part of business growth."

At least once a year take a step back and evaluate all of your relationships, milestones, and challenges. Consider who has had an impact on your business, both from a growth perspective and a challenge perspective. There's a lot of value in doing this kind of assessment. Once you know who has had a positive impact on your business you can set out to acknowledge their contribution. At the same time, if you identify people who have had a negative impact on your business growth you need to make some decisions on whether you should continue to interact with them moving forward.

There are a lot of possible groups of people who can impact your business. There might be employees. There most likely will be vendors, clients, resources, and referral partners.

Feeling and expressing gratitude is a huge part of business growth. And it is one of those things that requires a system. In the United States, November is traditionally the time when you count your blessings and focus on those things and people you're grateful for. However, when it comes to business, there's no wrong time to show your gratitude. I believe that it shouldn't be just once a year! I think we should always focus on the things in life and business that we are thankful for. Then take it one step further and create a program for expressing your gratitude year-round.

From a business standpoint, you can appreciate all of the people and organizations that help you reach your goals. Who are those people? They are your clients, suppliers, referral sources, partners, contacts, and, if you have them, your employees. When you think about it, there are a lot of people who help buoy you up; help you stay on course; help you grow.

You should be showing your gratitude all year long. And the great thing is that you can start any time! Showing appreciation during unusual times can have a greater impact than doing it during traditional times like November and December. Create a system for how you want to thank your various supporters and stick to the plan.

Be mindful that everyone likes to be acknowledged and feel appreciated. It's an easy thing that can have a significant impact.

There's a multitude of ways to reach out and thank people. You might decide to do the same thing for everyone. You may decide to have different programs for the different categories. Whatever you decide to do, make sure it's something you can do effectively.

Please Note: while you may use the same program, each touch should be unique to that person.

Some suggestions are: handwritten notes thanking them specifically, a phone call, a small token of appreciation, a book that has some meaning to the person, a referral, a connection.

Notice a thread here? The way you thank people should be individualized. It should have value and meaning to that person. You're trying to let them know you appreciate THEM specifically.

So, part of the HOW is really knowing these people. Get to know the people in your business world and find out what matters to them. Take some time and visit with the people in your world who have had an impact on your business. Find out what's going on with them, what their needs are, what matters to them. Then go out and take action on one of those items.

You're letting them know you appreciate them by taking the time and interest to get to know them better. You're then taking it one step further by taking action on what you learned.

When you appreciate others, they'll appreciate you. That appreciation will create an environment where they'll want to help you grow—whether through increased business, referrals, connections, or something else.

Could you build your business without those people—the clients, the referral sources, the connections, the suppliers? I don't think so. Do your business a favor and let them know how much you appreciate them working with you to help grow your business.

In addition, when you focus on gratitude, you aren't focused on selling. Yea! The relationships you build are better, deeper, and more meaningful.

Productivity Is Better Than Activity

---

*"Proactive, clear solutions will help you ensure
productivity instead of mere activity."*

So often salespeople find themselves working hard but not
accomplishing much. In my view, there's a lot of activity but
not much productivity. Having sold, and coached salespeople for
many years, I've identified some reasons why this is happening
as well as some solutions.

The first reason is not having a clear target. When you
believe that everyone is a potential client you dilute the pool and
your process. "**Everyone**" is not a potential client because many
people don't need or want what you have to sell. Still others
aren't in a position to buy what you have to sell. Moreover,
when you try to sell to everyone, your message gets lost and no
one hears it. Lastly, it's impossible to identify what's working
and what isn't in regard to your marketing efforts.

Instead of trying to prospect to everyone, pick a target market and focus on the message to them. What do they need? How do they receive information? What is the best way to connect with them to engage in the discovery process?

Another reason salespeople often engage in a lot of activity that isn't productive is they don't have a clear process. Here's what happens. They start to prospect and make appointments. They're going on those appointments and preparing proposals. They either get so busy with this that they drop their prospecting, or they think they should stop prospecting. After all, if they win these sales, they won't be able to handle more; better not prospect until they've gotten these sales under their belt. The problem? Until they have something, they don't have it! Banking on the potential won't put money in their account. Also, when they drop their prospecting, they create gaps in their potential and a lot more work in the long run.

Develop a clearly defined and specific process for prospecting and selling. Everything from cold calling to following up should be included. When you have a consistent process, you don't have to think about it. You can put the activities on your calendar and work the process.

Lastly, if you don't have clear measurement of your progress, you can find yourself being very active but not productive. You go, you do, you move along, and you never stop to take a look at how it's really going. This is really typical and unfortunate. You end up spending a lot of time doing things that are unproductive without realizing it.

Make sure your process includes goal setting and reviewing. How many sales and how much revenue do you want to achieve? As you work your process, keep an eye on how well you are reaching those goals. Make changes where you need to. One review process I like is the 30/4 Review Program. Set an appointment on your calendar every 30 days to engage in the following:

Run a report on your progress. Review that report and ask yourself these questions

1. What worked? During the past 30 days, which practices, programs, activities worked in helping you get to goal?
2. What didn't work? Which things didn't help you get to goal?
3. Did you hit your goal? Were you able to achieve your 30 day goal? Did you exceed it? Did you fall short?
4. What do you need to do for the next 30 days? This is where you determine your plan for only 30 days. You'll keep the things that worked, change or eliminate the things that didn't work, and move forward.

These proactive, clear solutions will help you ensure productivity instead of mere activity. You will seize many more sales this way.

Resources

Visit www.SeizeThisDay.co/resources
for downloadable versions of these resources

Resource A

WHY PEOPLE BUY WORKSHEET

_____

_____

_____

_____

_____

_____

What is your differentiator? (why you/your company)
Note: great customer service is not a differentiator!

_____

_____

_____

_____

_____

Resource B

TOP CLIENT CHARACTERISTICS WORKSHEET

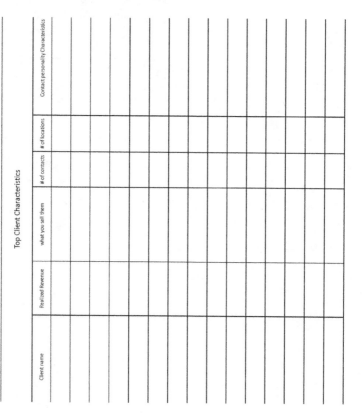

Resource C

TOP CLIENT ORIGINS WORKSHEET

N = Networking	CC = Cold Calling	PS = Public Speaking
R = Referral	DM = Direct Mail	T = Tradeshow

Client	Acquisition Method

Resource D

---

30 Second Introduction Options

I am passionate about _____(Action word)_____ _____(Target Market)_____
_____(do what?)_____ so they can _____(result)_____

I change the lives of _____(Target Market)_____ by helping them
_____(do what?)_____. My clients _____(result)_____

My clients realize _____(result)_____ through the programs/products I
provide them. Together we _____(Action word)_____ so they can
_____(value)_____

I spend most of my time _____(Action word)_____ with _____(Target Market)_____.
Together we _____(do what?)_____ that allow them to
_____(do what?)_____. This results in _____(result)_____

Or, create your own with the following attributes:

Who you are _____

Who you work with _____

The value you bring _____

With what result _____

153

Resource E

Discovery Meeting Questions Worksheet

Do you anticipate any challenges achieving the goal(s)?

Do you have a timeline you are working with for these plans?

Have you ever worked with a company like ours before?

> If yes – how did that go?
>
>> What did you enjoy about the process?
>>
>> Was there anything you'd do differently in the future?
>>
>> What do you look for in an external partner?
>
> If no – have you ever considered it?
>
>> If yes – what were the factors that contributed to the decision not to move forward?
>>
>> If no – continue with the regular list of questions

What is the decision-making process in your company? (this should include who, how, timeline). If they don't tell you who, ask – could you share with me who is involved in the decision making?

I wouldn't ask them what role they play in the process. The goal of asking questions this way is to keep them from going on defense. You just want to gather information.

What, if anything, has changed in your industry in the past 5 years?

Are there changes you are anticipating in the coming years?

Are there other areas of the company that could benefit from learning about our unique approach to (what you offer)?

Would you be open to introducing me to someone in those areas?

Have you considered a budget for this? If they've used a product or service like yours in the past they have an idea of what the investment could be. So, frame the budget question based on whether they've had experience before.

Resource F

E-Newsletter & Social Media Posting Worksheet

E-Newsletter

You can choose to have up to 3 sections

First few sentences from blog post with 'read more' link that takes the reader to the blog

Client or employee highlight with photo

Product/service information – this can link to the website page where they can learn more

For the first section, write a blog post, put it on your website, then you can use the first couple of sentences for the e-newsletter.

Each section should have an image and all images should be linked to the website

Send out the e-newsletter once a month. Some industries will lend themselves to more frequent emails. Restaurants with weekly specials are one category. Think about your audience and what they want to know. An e-newsletter should be informational and engaging.

Have a sign-up opportunity on your website, Facebook page, and anywhere you're engaging with people. Let everyone know you have a newsletter. However, do not automatically sign people up for the e-newsletter when you meet them. You only want people who want to receive the emails.

You can create separate lists by audience. You can have a list for one type of customer, a list for companies, a list for a specific interest, etc. All of these people can be on the main list. The reason for having separate lists is so you can send emails directly to an audience about specific information. It's direct marketing.

Social Media Posting Schedule

1. Decide what you want to be sharing and when
2. Decide when you'll post to each platform (Facebook, Instagram, etc.)
3. Create a calendar for posting or use a program like Buffer to schedule www.buffer.com or www.hootsuite.com
4. Use google alerts to pull content to you that you can share www.google.com/alerts

Try to post directly to the platform whenever you can. Monitor your newsfeeds and comment on what other people are sharing. On your business pages ask engaging questions. The goal is to get people to respond and interact with your posts. That will get you in front of their connections.

Using a blog on your website as the anchor for your content helps you accomplish a couple of goals. First, it continually drives people to your website. Second, it gives you the opportunity to repurpose the content on your other social media profiles.

Resource G

Prospecting Script Worksheet

1. Select a target market

2. Create a list of companies in that target

3. Look on LinkedIn to see how you are connected to them

   a. Direct connections – if you find someone you're directly connected to then email him or her about having a short meeting so you can learn more about what's going on with them.
   b. Someone in common – when you find someone who is a 2nd connection take a look at who you have in common.

If it's someone you know well, reach out to YYOUR connection and say, "I see you're connected to Joe Smith. Would you feel comfortable introducing me to him? I'd like to learn more about his business. I might have a program that could be valuable for him. It might not be. Learning about his business will give me some insights into where he is."

Or simply

"I see you're connected to Joe Smith. Would you feel comfortable introducing me to him? I'd like to learn more about his business."

When they say, "yes", say, "that's great. Could you do an email introduction? That way you'll have each other's contact information."

When you receive the email intro, you reply all and say, "thanks (contact name). Hello (prospect). So nice to meet you. Would you be available for coffee or a quick call? I'd like to learn about you and your business."

   a. In groups with them – these people are now 2nd connections. You can ask to connect directly with them through LinkedIn. To do this, go to their profile and click the connect button. When the box pops up choose the group option. In the box where you can put a message say, "Hello (contact name). We share (fill in the name of the group) group. I'd like to connect with you and learn more about your business. Sincerely, (your name)."

159

Once they accept your connection, you can grab their email address from their LinkedIn profile (in the contact info section). Send them an email that says, "Thank you for accepting my LinkedIn connection request. I'm wondering if we could schedule a short phone call or grab coffee so I can learn more about your business."

Take it from there. You're not meeting with them to sell them on your product/service. You're meeting with them to learn about their business FIRST. Then, if what they tell you coincides with what you offer, you can ask some questions to see if there's an opportunity there.

(Or you can ask about a specific day and time. For example, "how does Tuesday at 3 look for you?")

For those companies where you have no connection, you will have to do some form of cold calling. Sending an introductory letter with your brochure is a great first step.

1. Send a letter with a brochure and business card in an envelope with a handwritten address and real stamp, not something from the postage meter. Go to the post office and buy some stamps.

2. Put an appointment on your calendar to do the follow up call. Call to follow up 3-5 business days after you send the letter.

If you get them on the phone you can say:

"Hi {prospect}. This is (you) at (your company). I'm calling to follow up on the information I sent you a couple of days ago. Have you had a chance to take a look at it?

Is it something you'd be interested in exploring? I promise I'm not going to sell you anything! I'd simply love to learn more about your company. If we have a program that could help you, I'd be happy to tell you about it then. If not, I'll tell you that as well. How's next Tuesday at 3?"

If you get voicemail –

"Hi {prospect}. I'm sorry I missed you. This is (you) at (your company). I'm following up on some information I sent you a couple of days ago regarding (your solution).

I'd love to learn about the kinds of programs you have implemented at {name of company}. I'm not trying to sell you anything. I'm merely interested in learning about your company and (issues you resolve). There's the possibility that our program might be a good addition. Or not. Either way, I always find value in meeting other business leaders in the community. I'll send you an email with the same information from this voice mail, in case that's your preferred communication method.

Please feel free to reach out at xxx-xxx-xxxx if you'd like. I'll follow up with a call in a couple of days to try to connect.

(Be sure to send that email detailing the same information.)

If they don't reach out to you, call them in 3-5 business days to follow up. You don't have to leave a voicemail the second time. But do put a note in your records that you tried. Try again in 3-5 business days. You get to decide how many times you are

going to try to connect with them by phone and/or email. When you reach the point where you think they aren't interested, you can either stop the outreach, or you can call one more time and let them know you are going to stop calling for now. You can say something like you are starting to feel like a pest and don't want to feel that way, so you're going to put a note in your calendar to check in a couple months from now. In the meantime, if they determine they'd like to talk, they can reach you at xxx-xxx-xxxx.

You can also say something like – "I get it if (your offering) is not something that is at the top of your priority list at this time. Please know you won't offend me if you tell me you don't want to meet. I appreciate that this isn't for every company. I certainly don't want to be pestering you, but I also don't want to assume to know your level of interest. I'll try you again in a couple of days unless I hear otherwise."

What to do in the meeting

Once you've secured a meeting date and time you want, be sure to be ready for it. Refresh yourself on any research you've done on the company. If you haven't done any, schedule time to research them online. The more you know about them the more you'll have to talk with them about.

You'll also want to have a list of questions to ask them in the meeting. Resource E is a start. You can download the list and add to it with the questions that are specific to the product or service you offer. Just make sure the list is as comprehensive as possible. You're on a discovery mission.

Once you have the answers to your questions, you'll know whether you can provide them with a proposal. Thank them for the information and offer to create a proposal.

"Thank you so much for taking time with me today and sharing so much information. Based on what you've shared, I think you might be able to provide you with a program that can result in improved {_____}. Can we schedule a follow up meeting when I can bring in the proposal and we can go over it?"

If you find from their answers that either you can't provide them with a proposal, or, they are not a company you want to work with, respond like this: "Thank you so much for taking time with me today and sharing so much information. I truly appreciate you allowing me to learn about your business. I don't want to take any more of your time. Based on what I've learned, I don't believe we are the best resource for you. Thank you. Have a good day."

If you're going to provide a proposal, go back to the office and create it. The beginning should be a recap of what you heard from them. The second section is the solution you're proposing. The last section is the details – their investment, amount of time, location, etc. When you take the proposal to the prospect, start by reviewing what you heard them say. "What I heard you say is this ... "

"Based on that information we propose to . . . . . . "

"How does that look?"

Remember, you can offer a pilot program so they can get an idea of what you can do for them before they sign on for a long program at a larger investment.

If you're not going to provide a proposal, then send them a handwritten note thanking them for their time.

Resource H

Sales Process Guide

Select your target companies

Use Google to find those companies that fit the target and make a list

Identify the contact in each company

Determine if you know the contact, or if you know someone who knows them well enough to provide an introduction

For those companies where you know someone other than the contact, ask for an introduction:

"Hi Joe. Would you be open to introducing me to {contact}? I'd like to learn about (your area of interest). We've created a product/service that might help them (solve the problem you address). Do you think that's something they'd be interested in exploring?"

For those companies where you know someone who knows a leader at the company, ask for an introduction.

"Hi Joe. I understand you are connected to (contact). Would you be open to introducing me to him/her? I'd like to learn about (your area of interest). We've created a product/service that might help them (solve the problem you address). Do you think that's something they'd be interested in exploring?"

When you get the introduction, your goal is to gain a meeting. You reach out to the prospect by phone.

"Hello, {prospect}. I appreciate 'Joe' introducing us. I was wondering if we could schedule a short meeting. I'd love to learn about your company. We're all about (your solution) and we like to connect with other companies in the area. Is there a time next week that works for you?"

Resource I

_____

PROPOSAL TEMPLATE

Proposal for {Prospect Company Name}

Date: MM/DD/YYYY

RECAP

This is where you summarize what you heard the prospect tell you about their situation.

PROPOSAL

This is where you tell them your plan for helping them resolve their issue. You are responding to what they told you in the meeting. Your proposal must speak to their needs and wants in order to be effective.

DETAILS

Date:

Location:

Frequency

Financial Investment

Duration

Reporting

*Proposal expires 30 days from issuance

Resource J

TARGET MARKET DEFINITION WORKSHEET

Potential Markets	Why They Need The Product/Service	Buyer/User/Both

About The Author

Diane Helbig is an international business and leadership change agent, author, award-winning speaker, and podcast host. As president of Seize This Day, Diane helps businesses and organizations operate more constructively and profitably. Diane is passionate about guiding business professionals  through the challenges of planning and growing a business.

From strategic planning to sales training to communication, Diane provides expertise based on over 20 years of business leadership and sales experience. Diane's no nonsense, straightforward approach cuts through the noise and allows clients and training participants opportunities to realistically and enthusiastically implement the plans they devise.

Diane is the author of *Lemonade Stand Selling* and *Expert Insights*. She is the host of the Accelerate Your Business Growth podcast and the Business Growth Acceleration video channel.

Diane is the founder of the Business Opportunity Network, a business development program where business therapy meets growth.

Connect with Diane:

Www.SeizeThisDay.co

Www.LinkedIn.com/in/dhelbig

Www.Instagram.com/SeizeThisGrowth

Www.Twitter.com/SeizeThisGrowth

Ready, Set, Go!

Thank you for reading part or all of this book. I truly hope it provides you with guidance and information you can use in your business. The only thing left is to take action. Try one thing you've read, review its effectiveness, and go from there.

My goal in writing this book is to explore every aspect of sales and cover everything I've seen that works and doesn't work. I'm on a mission to improve the processes all sales professionals and small business owners use so they gain better results.

This book is about and for you. You can succeed without selling. You can enjoy the sales process. And you can realize success as you define it.

So, what are you waiting for?! Get going! And if you find you could use some help, please reach out. I'd be honored to work with you on your own individualized processes. My Sales Strategy Program is designed for just that purpose.

To your success!